THE
NEW
ERIE
CANAL

A Recreational Guide

by

John R. Fitzgerald

Maps and Cover Design by Robert Clancy

Illustrations by Paul E. Hook

QUEST PRESS

Copyright 1993

by

John R. Fitzgerald

Library of Congress Cataloging in Publication Data
Fitzgerald, John R.   1930-
The New Erie Canal,
includes index.
1. Erie Canal History
2. New York State Barge Canal, Cayuga--Seneca Canal,
Oswego Canal, Champlain Canal Description and Travel
Guidebooks
3. Historic Sites
Library of Congress Catalog Card Number: 9209349

ISBN 0963506102

For Patricia.

Because she says she knows why.

INTRODUCTION

This is a *recreational* guide describing interesting and significant places along the inland waterways of New York State. It's a "where-to" and "how-to", for people on boats, bicycles, automobiles and walkers on canalside trails.

A little history has been included to help make your travels meaningful and complete. Indeed, a book like this would be grossly incomplete without history. Not worth doing.

My hope too is that I have been able to impart a sense of the high spirits and unbounded optimism that ran rampant through this countryside in the days of the original Erie Canal. Perhaps I have overly romanticized those times and feelings. Perhaps. But if your memories are rich and often-recalled after travels along New York's water routes, then my enthusiasm will have been justified.

These waterways and lakes are now really physically independent of the canal. You can certainly bicycle, picnic on the shores or launch your boat, without any thought of a canal. In a more expanded sense than transportation. the canal is the spiritual cement that binds the waterways.

You can find your own kind of enjoyment along these waterways. The regions are all different, with their own special character. The western part of the Erie is largely true canal, cut through land, much like canalling in Europe, often removed from highway and railroad, intimate with its little towns and villages. The scenic eastern section is mostly river controlled by locks. The Finger Lakes, of course, are friendly, unintimidating, simply beautiful good-sized lakes. And it's impossible to travel the short spur to Oswego and Lake Ontario, at least for me, without sensing winter storms sweeping off Lake Ontario. Geology and weather leave their mark.

Transiting the Champlain Canal is to reach back into the earliest era of long-distance travel on this hemisphere.

And the Hudson River: crucible of our independence. Without this tidal estuary there would have been no ready access to the interior and no Erie Canal.

Most of the places I mention as worth visiting can be reached from the river, by a good stretch of the legs, a little bicycyle ride or through ingenuity, imagination and sweat. If a place is a cab ride away, I have tried to indicate it, but generally there is so much to see and do that THE NEW ERIE CANAL is pretty busy just keeping up with nice places close to the water.

This guide is meant to be definitive but not exhaustive and is mostly about places I have visited and personally know about, or know that they are worthy of your consideration.

There's information in here for boaters transiting the Atlantic--Great Lakes, and for summer sailors from anywhere seeking a low-key, soft-paced holiday through truly varied and often really beautiful scenery. Although the waterways pass through densely populated areas, the view from the river is rarely harsh.

Even on those short stretches of shoreline occupied by factories, the buildings have been around for so long that they can only be classified as industrial archaelogy. Virtually none of these structures function for their original purpose and are now mossy artifacts of our more recent commercial history.

Traveling the canal is an archaelogical field trip. This "new" canal is fairly old itself. Our ancestors' herculean efforts are little-noticed because the original canal has been so redesigned, rebuilt, reconstructed and relocated that you have to look sharply for its marks, now covered by turf, gravel, trees, shrubs, and downtown boulevards.

Life has moved away from the canal, eased out of the once vibrant villages and motored its way into urban complexes and shopping centers.

Boaters are not this enterprise's only constituents. I want these pages to help bicyclists, walkers, picnickers, fisherfolk, and picture-takers. I hope it can help to point out and enhance your enjoyment of historic sites, museums, small towns, big cities, restaurants, and just sitting around soaking up our rich atmosphere while watching the boaters, bicyclists, walkers, picnickers, fisherfolk and picture-takers.

All of the modern lock sites are accessible by automobile; many *are* parks, with picnic tables, charcoal grills and parking--great favorites of the local folks.

The idea tying all of this together is that these places are functioning parts of the canal system or accessible from it. If your boat is readily land-transportable, other possibilities are open: Lake George, all the other Finger Lakes, lakes throughout the Adirondacks, and on and on!

You can look on the inland waterways of New York State as a nice means of getting somewhere else, or you can simply regard these pleasant water routes and lakes as destinations in themselves.

Marinas and access to life's little amenities abound

Marinas and access to life's little amenities abound on the Hudson, Lake Champlain and Oneida Lake. The Finger Lakes too have marine facilities when and where you need them. The canal just doesn't have many marinas along its banks, or restaurants, or convenience stores. You'll never be seriously deprived for milk, bread, food and ice along the canals--just walk a bit to find the stuff.

There are plenty of restaurants between Albany and Buffalo, but they exist for four-wheeled travelers. I have only mentioned a few along the canal's right-of-way because as I went back to check them out I found great disparity from what I remembered on previous visits and what I found today. Perhaps my tastes had changed: living in New York City and San Francisco tends to prejudice ones' culinary proclivities. Therefore, although mention of a few restautants did creep in, I decided that this is a tourist's guide book and not Guide Michelin.

Also, to do justice to the many attractions of Lake Champlain and the Hudson River as complete cruising grounds, and to document all their marinas, restaurants, attractions, and anchorages is beyond the scope of this book. It would be three other books, all larger than this.

The conventional account is that New York State built the canal. I believe it's the other way around: the canal built New York State.

John R. Fitzgerald

Author's Note:

The English system of measurement is used throughout. Distances referenced on the canals are statute miles, but nautical miles are used on the Hudson River because that's the way NOAA does it on their charts. If elapsed time is used to describe the travel between two points, I have used 10 miles per hour. Elevations are noted in feet. Oftentimes, the term "canal" is used when I'm actually talking about a river, but that "river" is part of the canal system. In the course of several modernizations, New York gradually canalized several rivers, and shifted parts of landcut canal to river.

JRF

TABLE OF CONTENTS

Chapter I

View from the Water

Today's inland waterways in New York State are generally quiet, placid, tranquil and peaceful.

So peaceful, in fact, that it requires a powerful leap of the imagination to envision the constantly busy life and commercial activity that coursed these banks for over 100 years from the early 19th until the early 20th century.

There is so much *history* here that you can feel it. It is a palpable, real sense of all that has gone before and is one of the reasons the canal survives so strongly in our imaginations. There were many other canals in the country, but only this one has left such a vivid imprint on our historical consciousness.

Three main themes constitute the historical legacy of the canal: transit route to the American West; chief contributor to New York City's ascendency; the approximate geography and catalyst for an explosion of new religions, social experiments, political and economic schemes.

Today it may be even be difficult to imagine that the building of the original Erie Canal was one of the most intensely competitive activities in America.

It was competitive with another country, among cities of the Eastern Seaboard, among cities and towns along the route, between other states, and vigorously fought over community-by-community for construction contracts. It was the centerpiece for that most competitive of all activities--politics--for almost half a century.

Despite all the romanticizing about this canal that we have inherited, the real essence of the Erie was its thoroughly commercial character. If Americans know about the canal it is in the context of how history is taught in our schools--from a social, political, military or religious perspective. There is some discussion of economic history--causes and results of wars, immigration, social movements. But the "economic" content of history is as close as we come to business or commercial history.

The building of the Erie Canal was a hard-fought commercial battle. In a strictly business sense, the canal was probably the single most successful undertaking in the country. Most canals--and a lot were built--were not successful. The Erie was successful even before it was completed. By 1826 when the main line had been completed at a cost of $7,700,000, an income of $1,000,000 had already been realized from operations on the partially completed inner sections!

The idea of a canal was inherently competitive with Canada. Even before 1800, early explorers and travelers envisioned some sort of water route across North America. While Canada waited many years for a more ambitious ship canal, it missed a decisive moment in history when the great westward movement developed the rich mid-West. As heroic an undertaking as the original Erie Canal actually was for the time, it is a modest barge canal. But it was completed and it worked.

The war of 1812 was scarcely over before construction actually started; the nation's self-interest was at stake. One of our most serious problems during the war was supplying the "northwest" as we knew it then; it had cost $2000 to haul a $400 cannon from Washington to Lake Erie! Americans were starting to think of themselves as a country but Canadians had not yet formed a national identity. Nevertheless, this was a state-centered activity. New Yorkers, in their competitive urgency, thought first of their community, then the state, which finally made the canal possible when the Federal government did not support it. This then became a state effort, hard to imagine in these times when anything on remotely the same scale would either be a Federal project or not done at all. Nevertheless, the canal was totally nationalistic in character.

Even though New York City constituencies--financiers, artisans, but mostly labor--sided against the canal, its completion made the City a clear winner in a fierce competition with Philadelphia and Boston. Other states correctly anticipated the

2

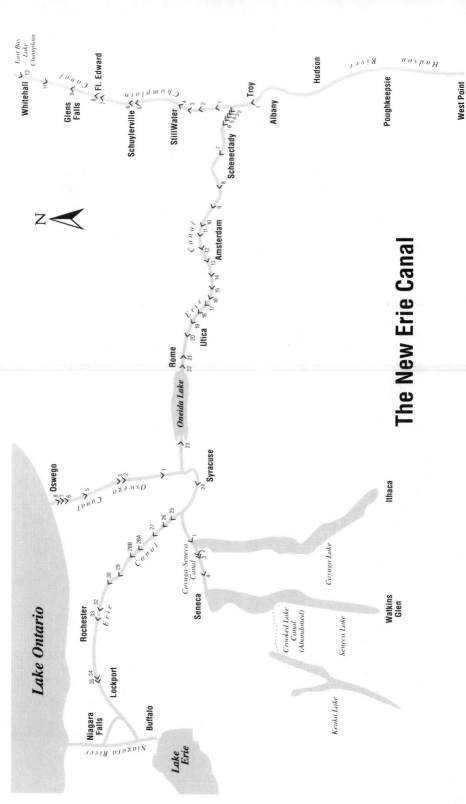

The New Erie Canal

trickle of westward expansion that started after the Revolution as the key to their prosperity. A canal was built across the Appalachians in Pennsylvania. Visit the ruins of the inclined planes (removing the vessel from the water, placing it on a wheeled carriage, and rolling it up a sloped railway while another barge descended on an adjoining plane to balance the weight) over the Alleghenys in Western Penmsylvania and you'll understand why that one was not successful. Yet, up to almost the last minute before construction started, there were schemes to design the Erie with inclined planes.

The Chesapeake & Ohio started westward from Washington to get at the coal of western Maryland. Ohio had extensive canals. Indiana wanted canals so badly that they damn near bankrupted the state. Others were started along the Atlantic Coast. In New York, canals were synonymous with political debate for over 50 years: improvements to the Erie, canals to the Finger Lakes, the Southern Tier, the Black River country, a connector to the Allegheny River.

Competition for the canal route within the state was just as determined as competition out of the state. One early proposal called for simply running a canal from western New York into Lake Ontario and then presumably floating down the St. Lawrence River. The St. Lawrence has a drop of 245 feet from Lake Ontario to sea level but--typical of the debate--such minor engineering impediments were often not considered germane to the argument. Still, because of the high cost of overland transportation, putting a barrel of Genessee flour on a Montreal dock was quicker and cheaper than sending it to New York. But it took much longer to get that Genessee flour to Europe via Montreal than by road and river to New York and thence overseas.

An 1808 survey greatly aided the cause of the east-west interior route all the way to Lake Erie. Even if it had been possible to construct a Lake Ontario--St. Lawrence canal, the benefits to New York State and access to world markets from New York City would never have been realized. There would have been a New York but its self-coronation as the "Empire State" would have been a hollow boast.

Cities and towns were very much part of the competition.

Selection of the site for the western terminus of the canal between Buffalo and Black Rock produced a real donnybrook. Name calling and local editorializing was just a small part of the competition. The Buffalo-Black Rock terminus decision drew its supporters into major State and National political battles. And now, few know about Black Rock, long part of "Greater Buffalo."

The award of construction contracts to build sections of the canal was not exempt from the competitive arena. Entrepreneurs competed for contracts on small sections--some even as short as one-quarter mile--of the canal. These home-grown contractors may not have had much previous relevant experience but they did have enthusiasm, ingenuity and resourcefulness.

When railroads started crossing the state only a few years after the canals had been completed, few competitive instincts stirred. New Yorkers in general were most interested in their own economic well-being. The canals were so successful that a sense of hubris surrounded their very presence. Railroads were regarded as another overall economic boost and--increasingly--year-round transportation. However, when the latest modernization of the canals into the Barge Canal was proposed, much of the support was largely an anti-railroad sentiment, even though serious doubts about the long-range viability of the canals existed. By then the railroads had alienated just about everybody except their owners.

Railroads generally followed the canal which, in spite of what originally seemed dramatic changes in elevation, was basically a water-level route. Railroads penetrating New York via the Erie Canal route had by the far the easiest route West, much easier than the dramatic and expensive switchbacks and tunnels made necessary crossing the Appalachians' steep grades farther South.

The rivers, canals and lakes in this guide all follow well-documented aborignal trade paths, heavily traveled for hundreds of years by foot and canoe. The Indians were prodigious travelers whose intimate knowledge of the land greatly eased European access into the interior, speeding colonization and hastening their own diminishment.

The areas covered by this book include five, six or seven distinct geographic regions, depending on how you want to classify them. There is great geologic diversity in this small part of the world: Adirondack, Green, Berkshire, Catskill, Helderberg, Palisades all contributing their imprint from radically different origins measured by the slow tick of geological time. As man has moved through this natural landscape, each region developed its own unique history, cultural nuances and economy.

Hudson River: This short but magnificent river is technically a tidal estuary from the Atlantic to the Federal Dam at Troy, about 150 miles north of Manhattan's 79th Street Boat Basin. No low bridges! It's the only stretch of New York's inland waterways where you will encounter ocean-going ships...and tides. On the western horizon you'll find authentically beautiful mountain scenery--Catskills, Helderbergs and Palisades--all the way from Albany to the George Washington Bridge. If you're sailing, step the mast and hoist the main!

The NYS Canalboat Governor Cleveland makes passage through the Waterford flight.

6

Champlain Canal: Following the Hudson River north from Albany, then into the earth-cut Champlain Canal puts you into the valley of Lake Champlain. This large lake is located between two of the major mountain ranges of the East, with New York's Adirondacks to the west and Vermont's Greens to the East. During the French and Indian Wars, the Revolution, and the War of 1812, the region saw much fighting, major troop movement, and decisive battles that changed the history of the world.

Oswego Canal: Although it is only 24 miles long, this section is a lot more than just the route from the main line to Lake Ontario. The Tug Hill Plateau starts its rise up to the Adirondacks just east of here. There is a slightly untamed, completely different feel to the countryside. The wildlife is wilder and there is more of it. (This is the only place I've ever spotted an eagle in New York.) Fishing is great--for smallmouth bass and walleyes in the Oswego River. Salmon lurk in abundance just below the mouth of the river...authentic world class fishing!

Finger Lakes: A short trip on the Cayuga--Seneca Canal puts you into Cayuga or Seneca Lakes. Cayuga, longest of the Finger Lakes, has Ithaca at its southern end (40 miles), superb fishing, four state parks, picnicking, spectacular walks, swimming--all those things that could happily consume an entire vacation. Historic Seneca Falls, birthplace of Women's Rights, is on the branch of the canal heading into Seneca Lake. There's Grand Prix Auto Racing and the Motor Racing Museum at Watkins Glen, great golf scattered all over these ridges, winery tours and tastings, and the lovely embrace of the Finger Lakes.

The Erie Canal: This is the original cross-state link, the "main line" that literally opened the west, brought prosperity to upstate New York, made New York City a power in world commerce, and created the synergy for some of the nineteenth century's most radical and original movements. I have divided it into four regions because of distances involved and because each deserves the focus of attention to highlight distinct characteristics. Going from east to west...

Capital District Region is a densely populated area with a practically limitless range of attractions for boater, bicyclist, picnicker, city buff, shopper and historian. It is here that the Erie Canal proper actually begins (or ends?). The entire area is tied together with a complete network of bicycle paths. Boating can range from tranquil, along the Mohawk, to exciting--negotiating the first set of five locks that lift from just above sea level on the Hudson to 184 feet on the Mohawk.

Mohawk Valley Region brings you through one of the most beautiful valleys on the river. At times you are close enough to the foothills of the Adirondacks that you can actually see them peeking through on the northern horizon. If you are one of those folks with an intuitive-practiced inner sense for land forms, you can feel the presence of the mountainous mass over a near horizon. Much early colonial and Revolutionary history here. By the time you have passed through the area and enter into Onieda Lake, you are into the...

Central Region, aptly named for central New York, true "upstate", right in the middle of the canal. A side trip to Onondaga Lake and Syracuse should be certain to include the Canal Museum, greatly enhanced over the last few years. This section includes the branches to Oswego and the Finger Lakes. Near Palmyra there are historic sites of the Church of Jesus Christ of Latter Day Saints, and the Hill Cumorah pageant.

Western Region travels through many delightful smaller towns, engineering masterpieces of the original canal, access to Rochester, great biking and walking routes, and to the Great Lake for which the whole enterprise was named. The attractions are many: urban, rural and scenic, good restaurants, charming inns and an area where the canal is a noticeable, integral part of the community.

Chapter II

Immersed in History,
Politics and Engineering

Any trip along these waters is to immerse yourself in the social, political, commercial, religious and military history of the region, State and country.

There is no way to avoid history along this ancient transportation corridor. Even traveling the highly efficient New York State Thruway you can read the Department of Education historical plaques at the rest stops; the experience may be as sanitized as you might get at a theme park, but it's still history and it's all around you.

Boating the Erie and traveling its parallel roads puts you literally--physically--on Indian canoe routes, portages, colonial corduroy toll roads and the legendary Erie Canal itself. The slower you travel, the more you can absorb. That should make boating, biking and walking the preferred mode for the sensitive traveler.

The success of the Erie Canal was mostly timing. Location was important, but the Erie came in a window of time when the demand for moving people and goods was high and the steam engine had not yet developed the efficiency to make railroads practicable. Other canals on the Eastern seaboard and in the mid-west, started in emulation of the Erie's success, died early because steam propulsion had increased in efficiency and railroad locomotives could carry sufficient fuel on board to increase distances between re-plenishing. The seasonal limitations of canals in this part of the world with deep freeze winters obviously inhibited their competitiveness too.

The Erie established its franchise before the age of railroading, upgraded itself based on initial success, and was able to continue as a freight hauler for over 100 years.

The Erie was technologically compatible with its times and native resources in other ways too. Here was a modest ditch-- forty feet wide and four feet deep--that could be constructed by farmers turned contractors, using mostly local labor.

The first phase of canal building from 1817 to 1826 that saw the completion of the original Erie has received the most attention in our popular histories. It was marked by fierce politics, native engineering ingenuity, wild enthusiasm and immediate success. The second phase started only a decade after the completion of the original main line. It was really a thorough rebuilding, meant to correct the deficiencies of the original Erie and provide for even greater growth and accompanying prosperity. The original Erie was sufficient for the needs of New York State but a larger channel was needed for dense, high volumes of through traffic. The first rebuilding increased the canal's dimensions to 70 feet wide and 7 feet deep, with 110 by 18 foot locks, almost twice the size of the orginal. This phase too was bitterly contested in State politics but was solidly planned and "built to last." And indeed it did last...until the modern Barge Canal, with an earth channel of 160 by 14 feet, supplanted it in the early 20th century.

Some histories speculate that the Dutch, coming from a country that moved on man-made water routes, immediately sensed the potential of canals.

The French came through the same valleys, at about the same time, but were interested in furs and faith. Preaching and trading for pelts could be supported by canoe and bateau; there did not seem to be an unlimited commercial vision of the future.

Seasonal river navigation was an important element in penetrating the interior for the colonials. The impetus for westward movement existed all along the Eastern seaboard before the Revolution but white settlement west of the Appalachians was prohibited by a British-Indian accord.

New York had a sizable body of loyalists during the Revolution and bloody, often cruel Tory/Indian attacks on settlers kept the frontier in turmoil. As the Continentals became organized, armies under Sullivan and Clinton marched across the interior of New York, attacking and burning the villages of British-allied Iroquois. There was often a practical incentive for Continental soldiering: at war's end they were to receive land for service and here was a chance to scout the territory.

Settlement came quickly after the war. Yankees from New England arrived looking for land, easier-to-work acreage than their rocky thin soils. New York's new farms proved productive, lakes and streams were full of fish, and virgin forests provided unlimited quality timber.

But it was a long way to market and the roads were impossible.

One result, for instance, of the cost of transportation exceeding profit potential was the growth of the whiskey industry. Grain distilled into whiskey was valuable enough to be transported for a profit but bulk grain was not until the development of canals and railroads.

The first serious attempt at improved water transportation was started in 1792 by two privately owned stock companies, the Western Inland Lock Navigation Company and the Northern Inland Lock Navigation Company. The Northern company was chartered to develop a canal to Lake Champlain, but did not realize any success and was soon out of business. Western was to develop a water route from Albany to Lake Ontario and Seneca Lake, by way of the Mohawk River and Wood Creek. For over ten years they fought shortages of engineering knowledge, skilled labor, and funds. Despite many operational problems, the canal did function to some extent. Published historical accounts, however, do not acknowledge residual experience that logically would have been utilized in planning the Erie. Perhaps the technical experience--particularly feeder water and lock design-- was not put to use but the detailed knowledge of the route must have helped the Erie's designers. Later, the prominent stockholders were able to salvage some of their investment by selling out to the State when the Erie was authorized. The State, interestingly, was among the investors in the Western Company, made an initial gift, and later a loan.

One of the most substantial elements in the wide-ranging discussions of the day was an 1809 report to the Surveyor General, Simeon DeWitt, prepared by James Geddes, a young judge and surveyor from Onondaga County. Geddes surveyed from the Mohawk River, both the "Ontario" route from Oneida Lake to Lake Ontario and the "interior" route to Lake Erie. The "interior" route would have avoided scaling the daunting cliffs around Niagara Falls, a project that many thought difficult if not impossible but which had strong political advocates: the politically powerful Porters, owners of the route around Niagara.

The interior route seemed practicable after Geddes' discovery that it would be possible to span the Irondequoit Valley with some ambitious construction, and to cross the waters of the Genessee. Without driving a stake but with a surveyor's practiced eye, his discovery of a series of ridges over the difficult area would make the whole project eminently feasible.

Central to the debate of Ontario vs. interior was that many feared goods afloat on Canadian waters would keep on floating...down the St. Lawrence to Montreal and deny the benefits of commerce to New York. As the War of 1812 neared, some thoughtful politicians realized that Genesee farmers and other Western New Yorkers just wanted markets...even if those markets happened to be in Montreal!

Federal support had been sought for construction of the canal almost since the idea became something more tangible than ephemeral concept. George Washington supported the idea ever since he traveled the length of New York after the Revolution. Federal support for New York canals came tantalizingly close before the War of 1812. Canal boosters received some encouragement in 1807 when Secretary of the Treasury Albert Gallatin proposed a vast national program of internal improvements including canals around Niagara Falls, from the Hudson River to Lake Champlain, and from the Hudson to Lake Ontario at Oswego. One of Gallatin's proposals budgeted three million dollars for a canal from the Hudson to Lake Erie. Although Thomas Jefferson, president at the time, was a canal advocate in general, he did not support New York's and never saw funding for his favored Chesapeake & Ohio. Later, President James Madison did forward a proposal to a lukewarm Congress for New York canals. Neither legislation nor a Constitutional Amendment resulted as the Federal government became increasingly preoccupied with foreign relations leading up to the war. New Yorkers finally had to conclude that their State alone would have to build the canal.

Those years of high hopes for higher assistance, however, did help to spur planning and more in-depth discussion.

The war slowed down, but did not altogether halt, planning for a canal. Securing committments for land along the proposed right-of-way from large holders continued but DeWitt Clinton, mayor of New York City and the canal's most steadfast advocate, saw his influence diminished because of his anti-war stance. Clinton's politics, ambitions, and accomplishments centered on the canal. He was a difficult man in many ways but thoroughly altruistic and completely committed to his causes. To study his biography is to understand the birth of the Erie Canal. In 1816, heading a committee of prominent New Yorkers, he prepared his famous Memorial to the State Legislature that became probably the most influential of over thirty such petitions. Full of technical content and financial projections, its language nevertheless soared when alluding to the benefits and coming prosperity to be bestowed by the canal. Over 1,000 copies were printed and the document acted as the catalyst it was intended to be. Meetings were soon being held all over the state to discuss this latest in a long succession of canal proposals. But this time a new sense of urgency prevailed and soon the matter of the canal was again before the legislature.

Several major decisions dominated final debate. Two of the most contentious were final routing and the hard-to-kill idea of inclined planes versus locks. Arguments about route were inextricably enmeshed in political, local and special interest but the "interior" route was finally selected over the "Ontario" proposal. Proponents of inclined planes were stubborn, clinging to their favored design right up to the last minute even though the lock advocates thought that they had repeatedly discredited the idea. The decision favoring locks was unquestionably the right one, proving that politicians can make wise engineering choices.

One of the most strategic considerations in the War of 1812 had been control of the waterways--or at least the travel routes--proposed for the canal. A great surge of national expansion was ready to break loose once the war was over. Western expansion was going to take place whether or not a canal across

New York was built. With that spirit in the air--but also with hints of the recession that was soon to follow--a section of the canal from Utica on the Mohawk River to the Seneca River and 22 miles of the Champlain Canal from the Hudson River to Lake Champlain was finally approved by the Legislature in 1817. The political battles leading up to this conditional, virtually experimental, sectional authorization, were titanic. Although the legislative mandate was incomplete, work on the canal was ready to start. From 1816 on, the mood, attitude and sense of the State was that there would be a canal, even though it was never a political certainty.

As the early stages of what would become almost uncontained enthusiasm for the canal began to take hold, DeWitt Clinton--political identity virtually one with the canal--was elected Governor.

Ground was broken in Rome on July 4, 1817 for the long flat first section from just below Utica to the Seneca River. The soil was fairly easy to move and there were only six locks to be constructed. It was rationalized that even if no further construction ever happened benefits would be realized from a short functioning canal in that easy-to-build location.

More than 50 contractors were soon at work on awards as short as one-quarter mile. Local businessmen, farmers, artisans and mechanics were able to bid, complete, receive final payment, and bid on another section. Monthly progress payments were made in person by Myron Holley, Treasurer of the Canal Board of Commissioners, from a strong box in his horse-drawn carriage as he traveled the construction route. Holley paid in small bills drawn on local banks, further benefitting the immediate economy. Despite the many stories about Irish labor, most workers were recruited locally. In 1819--about half way through the first construction--it was recorded that three quarters of the work force was native born.

The entire enterprise was overtly nativist in structure and sympathy. These sentiments were most notable in discussions concerning design and engineering. Indeed, there was an aversion among the canal's early directors to learn from the French, who had already proven themselves prodigious canal builders, but

14

Relics of the 1842 rebuilding can be seen a few paces from Lock E-2 in Waterford.

a willingness to learn from the British, whose canal accomplishments were fine for England but less notable than the French. There seems to have been a subtle undercurrent of distrust: the "foreigners" were not quite to be trusted. English speakers were just less foreign!

Several histories claim that the canal became a school of engineering. It has even been called "America's first school of engineering." In a sense, that's true because there were no schools of engineering in the United States, but the boast is pretentious and claims too much. It's doubtful if the canal was much different than any other technically oriented industrial enterprise in accelerating the development of professinal engineering. There were no "graduate" engineers; they were all self-made. Engineering at the time had only two branches: civil and military. A young man would typically start out with a survey party cutting brush, driving stakes, holding the backsight and the level rod, measuring with the chain, manning the foresight, taking notes, learning trigonometry, operating the level and transit, doing calculations, and preparing plats and maps. Depending on ability and disciplined self-study, an engineer might emerge several years later. The development path for a self-made engineer as practiced on the canal in the early 1800's carried on until only recently--especially in civil, mining, structural--when a rigid compartmentalization began to be introduced with the proliferation of various "technician" levels based on a two or four year degree. Thus, the contribution of the canal in developing promising talent into engineers was no different than the typical career path widely followed up to the last generation or so in many other industries where the ranks of graduate engineers were supplemented by practical engineers trained on the job. Many of these practical engineers were able to append the coveted P.E. to their name after completing rigorous self-study programs and successfully passing the Professional Engineer exams.

Native ingenuity applied to the construction was often highly original. Two devices were especially effective: a tree extractor and a stump-puller. The tree remover was a fairly small machine that utilized the principles of lever and screw. The stump-puller was mounted on 16 foot wheels with a 30 foot axle to which was attached a 14 foot stump-pulling wheel, positioned over and connected by chain to the stump, with a multi-wrap of rope around the wheel giving an eight times power advantage so that oxen could make short work of even large stubborn stumps.

During the first season it was learned that plowing and then scraping was infinitely faster than spade and wheelbarrow. Wet clay soils still required manual digging but a lighter, easier-to-dump wheelbarrow was developed that greatly aided and speeded up the task.

Essential building materials were developed locally too. Something called "blue mud of the meadows" was able to prevent seepage when applied to the canal's walls.

One of the most significant discoveries was a limestone from Madison County that could be made into an effective underwater cement. This was the work of a young assistant engineer, Canvass White, who had just returned from extensive travels in Britain observing their hydraulic works.

No sooner would a section of canal be watertight than use began. Farmers became boat builders and judges became contractors. Despite financial, political and physical difficulties, completion of the middle sections between Utica and Montezuma swamps generated increasing enthusiasm in the planned, more difficult, but still unfunded western and eastern reaches. Finally, in April 1819 the Legislature authorized the Erie's completion. The ensuing political battles deciding just what parts would be completed and in what sequence were as titanic as the engineering scope and scale of the enterprise. And all this in the milieu of an election for governor.

Going into the election, many New York City constituencies still worried that the canal threatened their interests and would somehow remove the center of trade to the interior. Governor Clinton, with shaky political alliances but riding a wave of popular support for the canal, won re-election. In the process of the election Clinton's bitter enemies, whose politically opportunistic advocacy for the canal had been off-again-on-again became unwavering canal supporters.

Along with advocating much-needed constitutional reform and with the fervor of the newly converted in their support for

17

the canal, this "Bucktail" wing of the Republican party subsequently crafted a devilish legislative coup that removed Clinton from his position as Canal Commissioner as the canal neared completion.

The wrath of the voters was ferocious.

Despite Clinton's crippling political liabilities his support of, and identification with, the canal was so powerful in the voters' mind that he was again returned as Governor--to be serving as the State's chief executive when the canal was completed.

Following the completion of the first "experimental" section, the next phase called for extension to Rochester in the west and from Utica to Little Falls in the east. Backers of the interior route pushed for western construction as fast as possible to thwart any lingering impulse to resurrect the Ontario route.

During the early years of construction, the country was in a depression and the Panic of 1819 caused widespread economic hardship. Increasing expenditures on the canal, however, enabled those communities on its flanks to get along handsomely. And that was in a time before the concept of pump-priming was developed as a counterweight to hard times. The prevailing attitude seemed to be: Let's finish the canal and we'll all prosper.

By the time of the Marquis de Lafayette's visit to the United States in 1824 as a guest of the nation, he was able to tour an almost-completed canal. Final rock cuts were being made west of Lockport, and long sections had been in operation for several years. The French hero of the American Revolution had been through the south, west of the Mississippi, and up the Ohio Valley to Lake Erie, then to Buffalo where his festive tour started. Over 2000 boats already were working; 8000 men and 9000 horses employed. The celebrations honoring LaFayette were a preview of the grand parade down the canal that followed a year later.

On October 26, 1826 the Seneca Chief of Buffalo, with the canal's own hero and alter-ego Governor DeWitt Clinton aboard, became the first boat to make the through journey to Albany and then to Sandy Hook off New York City for the famous Wedding of the Waters ceremony. Clinton and his party of notables were toasted and entertained at principal stops along a festive right-of-way. Speeches were offered and returned at

18

every opportunity. The party started with the firing of cannon, repeated at the next locale in sequence down the canal all the way to New York City, to signal the completion of this mighty work.

The first Erie Canal was finished but the work would go on. More canals were to be built: the Cayuga & Seneca opened into those two Finger Lakes in 1828 followed in 1833 by a connector into the "Crooked Lake" Keuka; the Chemung to Elmira in 1833 along with a feeder to Corning; a five mile extension to Oneida Lake in 1835; Lake Ontario was finally reached via the Oswego Canal from Syracuse only two years after the Erie opened; the Chenango opened navigation in 1837 from the Erie at Utica down to the Susquehanna River; in 1837 Olean and the Allegheny River in southwestern New York was reached by the Genessee Canal; the Black River Canal was started in 1837 but not opened until 1851; the Champlain had started operation before the Erie itself! These were all ventures of the State. (The privately owned Delaware & Hudson ran from Port Jervis on the Delaware River to Kingston on the Hudson to deliver anthracite coal to New York City.) They all have a unique and fascinating history but most can no longer be reached by water-borne craft. That's part of the attraction to the Erie and its surviving connectors: with almost no freight being moved, it's a miracle that they are even floatable and accessible. To travel these canals today is truly to immerse yourself in history. You become part of a living legacy.

This is no theme park.

Canal Profiles

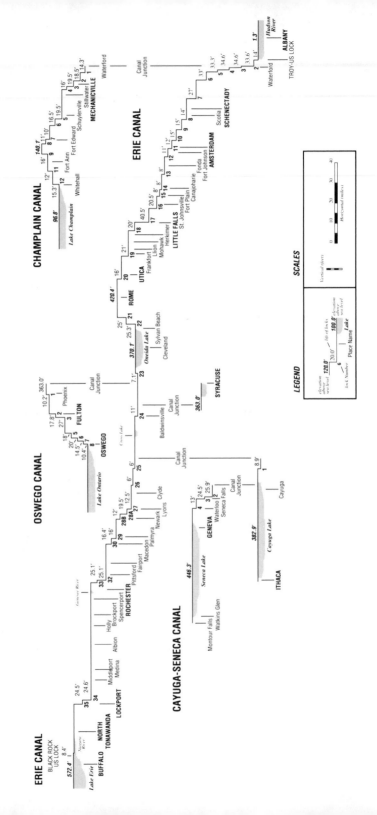

Chapter III

Getting Started: Boats 'n Bikes

Don't be dumb around water. You can have such a great time just being there, but first you must be sure that you know what you're doing and that your craft is ship-shape.

Here are some of the ways to learn about life on the water:

Read a book...try Chapman's Piloting, Seamanship and Small Boat Handling.

Go out with friends on their boat; grow up with a boating family or join the Sea Scouts.

Join the Coast Guard.

Attend Power Squadron or USCG Auxiliary courses.

Even if you do the first three, it's more than just a good idea to take the courses conducted by the Power Squadron or by the Coast Guard Auxiliary. Most of the instruction is conducted during winter evenings for a small fee that usually just covers the cost of materials. Programs range from 6 to 13 weeks. The best way to find out what is being offered in your area is to call the Foundation for Boating Safety at 800-336-BOAT. They'll give you the name of a local co-ordinator. If you are lucky enough to live in Upstate New York, some extra sessions are often appended to the instruction to cover negotiating locks.

Passage through the locks is not difficult but mastery of your boat should have been accomplished long before your first lock. There is a procedure involved--certain steps that must be observed. Your craft must be under control at all times and a degree of seamanship, particularly proficiency in line handling, is needed. Have your fenders out and lines ready. Most boaters on the canal run with fenders out on both sides--many with wear-boards outboard of the fenders--all the time. Practical perhaps, but unseamanlike to the eye of a blue water sailor. (English and French canalers also run with fenders always hanging out.) It's the skipper's responsibility to be certain that the crew knows how to execute assigned individual tasks. Commands should be precise and voiced with authority. Vocabulary is important:

everyone on board should know what the words mean. It doesn't have to be port and starboard, forward and aft, topside or downbelow--some people think all that salty talk is silly and pretentious anyhow.

A good cap (more salty talk--otherwise known as captain, skipper, Mom or Dad) is not belligerent but absolutely can't be tentative either. When it's time to leave, "cast off" means let go of that line (also known as a "rope") that's holding the boat to the shore whether it's on the bow (up front is OK too) or in the stern (back there is acceptable). AND DO IT NOW.

Know what to expect before arriving at a lock for the first time...especially the lift. The Recreational Map and Captain's Log provided by New York State both give the height of lift. The Log also provides lock and lift bridge phone numbers and distances measured from the Federal dam at Troy. The Captain's Log to the Barge Canal is available from New York State, Waterways Maintenance Division, 1220 Washington Avenue, Building 5, Room 216, Albany, NY 12232. (518) 457-1187. If you specifically ask, you can also obtain lists of tour boats and marinas, and a simple map of connecting waterways. An excellent publication, Recreational Map and Guide to NEW YORK STATE CA-NALS...Erie, Champlain, Oswego, Cayuga--Seneca can be obtained from NYS Office of Parks, Recreation and Historic Preservation, Agency Building 1, Empire State Plaza, Albany, NY 12238. (518)474-0456

LOCKING

When approaching a lock you'll notice that there will be either a green, red or no light. If the light is green, your vessel may enter the lock. If red or no light is displayed, you are to lay off or make fast to the wall at a safe respectful distance and sound three blasts of your horn. Six flashes of red or green means to hang tight and wait.

Enter the lock chamber at slow speed on a green light. Follow the lock tender's directions. The State's advice has been to have two 100 foot lines. A boat hook is a good idea for fending off. A single line is all right for a small craft. Fenders out on both sides. The boat operator is expected to hold close to a wall while lock operations proceed--gates close, water level changes, gates open. Turbulence can be expected. In the higher lift locks a tremendous volume of water moves through the structure in an amazingly short period of time. One end of the line is made fast to the boat, runs around a cleat or bollard on the lock wall and the other end runs free, to be taken up or paid out as the water level changes. The free end of the on-board handling line can be run through an open cleat for leverage and ease-of-handling. Stand by to free the lines and proceed ahead in boat order when the new level is reached and the mitre gates open. Be sure to keep the free end of a line neatly coiled and ready to pay out or take up. It is more than just being neat and seamanlike--tangles can be dangerous.

A handling line can also be run through the narrow metal ladders recessed into lock walls if your boat is positioned close-by. Just run a doubled bight through a rung...easy.

Lock tenders--particularly on the high lifts--don't look kindly at crews using a boat hook to maintain position at a ladder. The head of the boat hook could snap off or become disengaged if water unexpectedly surged in the chamber, perhaps tossing the unlucky craft onto another boat or smashing it into the wall. While rare, a surge can be caused if one on the huge internal valves suddenly failed. It may be all right to use a boat hook on the low lift locks but take the concerns of the lock tenders seriously; these are experienced people and they do know their lock.

Lately, the State has been installing pre-fixed lines at some locks. This is a fine idea and eases lock passage. The lines do get slimy and scumy after a while, just like the rest of the interior of the lock, so have some old gloves handy and something to wipe up with. These fixed-ropes are only attached at the top of the chamber wall. They hang free with a heavy weight attached to the lower end to prevent the lines from swinging wildly under water as the chamber is charged or discharged. With that heavy weight tugging below it takes a good little bit of strength to pull one of these lines aboard, especially if it's a high lift; don't assign a 10 year old to the job.

WHEN THE BOAT BUG BITES

If you were selecting a boat for use <u>only</u> on the canals, it would be long, skinny, simple and comfortable, with open fore-and-aft decks. That's what liveaboard canal boats look like in France and England where people have traveled those lovely waterways for hundreds of years. And that's the way Mid-Lakes Navigation and Collar City Charters--companies with boats-for-hire on the Erie Canal--have designed their boats. If you're taking your craft out into open water, or want to do some fishing, or are really most interested in sailing, or must trailer your boat every weekend, or only want to take day trips, or haven't much money, or a lot of it, then everything changes and the decision becomes just like the rest of life and very complicated.

Unless you have already owned several boats and have some opinions about yourself and boats, then don't rush out and buy something right away. I know it's tough <u>not</u> to buy because we Americans <u>know</u> that buying is our instant path to lower weight, reduced cholesterol, riches, a happier love life, snappier appearance, and an all-round guaranteed jolly good time. Start by picnicking at a canal park so you can watch the boats coming through, talk with some of the owners, visit a few boat yards, buy some boating magazines, finagle a way to actually cruise a little on the canal's waters. Every year new cruises are offered. These range from simple little trips for a few hours up to real voyages lasting several days or weeks. A list of cruise operators is contained in the Appendix.

Chartering is another solution to getting on the water with little investment and is perhaps the best of all worlds. Mid-Lakes Navigation and Collar City Charters mentioned above offer rental boats that look like they belong on the canal. Although patterned after English canal boats with an aesthetic tip of the hat to old time Erie Canal boats these specially-designed vessels are beamier than their English cousins, have a steel hull, bow thrusters and diesel engine. They are pleasing to the eye, reassuring to the nervous system, comfortable to live aboard and easy to drive. Mid-Lakes specializes in western New York and

Collar City in the east. Rates are very reasonable for the quality of the experience. For more information:
Mid-Lakes Navigation
11 Jordan Street, Box 61
Skaneateles, NY 13152.
(315)685-5722; (315) 685-8500

Collar City Charters
427 River Street
Troy, NY 12180
(518) 272-5341
Somewhere in this dreamy odyssey the boat bug might bite. You'll become hopelessly infected and only able to relieve your compulsive itchings by exercising your God-given right as a true American and buy something. The boat bug's bite is often more virulent than the bite of the new car bug. Tread softly. We're talking big bucks here.

TO DINGHY OR NOT TO DINGHY

One boat purchase that's easy enough is the dinghy, that is, if you decide that you need a dinghy. Throughout most of the canal it's easy enough to get ashore because there are walls at all of the locks and by many of the bridges. River sections have marinas, not evenly spaced, and not nearly enough. The Hudson River and all of the directly accessible lakes--Oneida, Cayuga, Seneca, Champlain--have marinas when you need them but you'll be more independent with a dinghy.

If you want to improvise, have flexibility in where you go ashore, poke around for old canal ruins and other adventures, it's great to have a small boat--rigid hull or inflatable--on board or towed. I'm partial to a canoe because they go fast and far, can get into just about anything faintly liquid, can be picked up and carried, and are fun to paddle. You have to know how to balance in 'em. It's not difficult but takes practice. Don't try transferring your groceries or bicycle to such a tippy platform until you know how to keep the creature docile.

Up and down the canals and connecting rivers you'll see

boats "anchored" with a line wrapped around an accommodating shore-side snag. That's OK, and if your hull can be snugged in close or run up a little, you can get to almost anywhere you really must reach on the canals.

Early in your boating career, learn the intricacies of real anchoring with an anchor. Don't think of the dinghy as a practical range-extender until you're proficient with ground tackle.

EFFICACY OF THE BICYCLE

The bicycle is another great low-budget range-extender. In France, the bicycle is an essential part of all canal boats--like engine, hull, wine, rudder, and helm. Remember, the French have almost 5,000 miles of canals and navigable rivers and they like to be admired.

The bicycle seems like such a natural adjunct to canal travel. Of course, it's useful for getting to the store, but on major stretches along and off to the sides of the waterway its recreational potential is especially endearing.

A well-developed bikeway follows the Hudson and Mohawk Rivers for 41 miles from Albany to Rotterdam Junction. Troy wants a 7-1/2 mile bikeway along its waterfront. There is a pretty 10 mile stretch from Amsterdam to Schoharie Crossing. An ambitious 66 miles from Schoharie Crossing to Oneida Lake is being explored and cleared for use as an unpaved trail by volunteers under the umbrella of the Mohawk Valley Recreational Task Force. A long trail from the Erie Canal Village on the outskirts of Rome to DeWitt on the outskirts of Syracuse has been opened for several years on the original Erie's tow path; a mountain bike can be pedaled here but it's not suitable for a road bicycle. Around Rome the trail appears to be little used but further west it gets quite busy at times.

Western New York has the longest existing range of bikeways and trails. Beginning in Wayne County and continuing around Rochester to Lockport there are trails designated on maps as "bikeways" but this is not a system or a network. Rather, it is a gradual running-together of locally supported trails and "bikeway" is to be taken figuratively: a mountain bike is generally OK but some sections are mostly for walking. Only around Rochester is the bikeway suitable for long continuous distances on a road bike. The trails are gradually reaching Buffalo but remember that this is all a bottoms-up development with inspiration and impetus coming from local communities. There is no central planning authority or direction. The only map available is of the Erie Canal Heritage Trail, a continuous section in Orleans and Monroe Counties, from the Niagara County line to Wayne County, and can be obtained from NYS Department of Transportation--Canals Unit, Region 4; 1530 Jefferson Rd., Rochester, NY 14623-3161. (716) 272- 3490. ᒐ 35-6250

The genuinelly outstanding bikepath system in the Capital District exists without any available maps. When the bikepath first came into operation the planning departments of Albany and Schenectady counties jointly provided a dandy Mohawk-Hudson Bikeway map, now long out of print and the planning departments are themselves hard to find. The bikepaths are wildly successful with the locals who know of their existence and

The end of summer--from Georgian Bay to Long Island.

27

where to get on and off. See the map at the beginning of Chapter IV; it will give you a good idea of the overall route and access.

Most trails have been developed on home-grown initiative, often with some local funding but almost always with State and Federal funding. New York State has never had any coherent overall coordinating strategy to document and publicize its canal trails so that tourists and out-of-towners could understand what is available. Descriptions in the geographic sections of this book should help.

The Bike Paths are not speedways. These paved by-ways are not for those fond of high-speed bicycling. You'll encounter hikers and walkers, bird watchers, baby strollers and tricycles. Some bicyclists will be poking along not much faster than the tricycles because they are there with the tricycles. Hard core bicyclists often eschew the Bike Paths for highways (hopefully with a wide clean shoulder) or Bike Routes, generally meaning a designated and marked corridor running on a roadway.

Chapter IV

*Capital District Region: Hudson River, Albany,
Troy, Cohoes, Erie Canal to Schenectady;
Locks 1 to 9*

The attractions of New York's capital city of Albany and
the nearby cities of the region are virtually endless. You'll find
fine and fancy dining, equally fine but not-so-fancy dining, year-
'round varied entertainment, fabulous shopping and old fashioned
touristing as good as it gets. The boating and biking are first
rate too.

Albany has special significance for a book like this.
Looking for a Northwest Passage near here in 1609, Henry Hudson
ran into rapids above what is now Troy. Albany was the setting
for the on-again, off-again political skirmishes involved in
establishing the canal, its extensions, new canals, and
modernizations.

We chose to start your trip here simply because so many
early immigrants started their trip into the interior here too.
Coming up the Hudson by steamer or sailing packet back in those
days was something of an extension of the ocean crossing itself.
Still at sea level, the tug of the world's tides could be felt all the
way to the end of navigation.

The approach to the interior did not yet seem irrevocable.

But at Waterford, the interior was abruptly introduced
by immediate passage through a series of locks, stacked almost
one on top of the other. Travelers with any money at all took
the three hour overland route to Schenectady from Albany to
board their first packet boat and avoided 24 hours on the water.
There was no choice for the poorest immigrants who payed a
penny a mile to travel on combination freight and passenger boats
of the line. Their sense of committment to a new land was
heightened by the almost constant lift of 27 locks over the first
30 miles of canal.

There is also something very appropriate about going

29

west from Albany.

Settlement started just about five years after Henry Hudson's visit of the Half Moon; within 15 years Dutch Walloons-- Flemish-- started the permanent settlement of Fort Orange. It prospered on the fur trade, pelts coming in over a network of well-developed Indian routes from throughout the Great Lakes. So many beaver skins came through that the community was called Beverwyck. The British called it Albany after they took over, in honor of the new owner, the Duke of Albany and York, later King James II.

Throughout the Hudson Valley, the Dutch instituted a feudal system of Patroonship, the patroon being awarded large land grants for settling 50 or more people. The patroons only leased land to the farmer holders, taking payment in "rents" of one-third the crop or in services. By the middle of the seventeenth century, the patroons of this area, the Van Rensselaers, held over 700,000 acres! This particular form of serfdom didn't end until 1846 when independent-minded Yankees enflamed the surrounding countryside with a genuine rebellion called the Rent Wars.

Albany was important because of location: the head of the water level part of the Hudson River; the base of the Champlain water route to Montreal; the eastern end of the Indian routes to the Great Lakes; and, later, the western terminus of the overland turnpike from New England.

The Hudson at Albany is really becoming a much cleaner river after

WATERFORD AREA

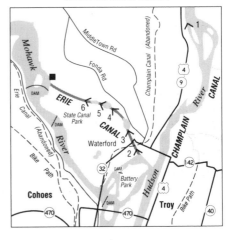

30

Capital District

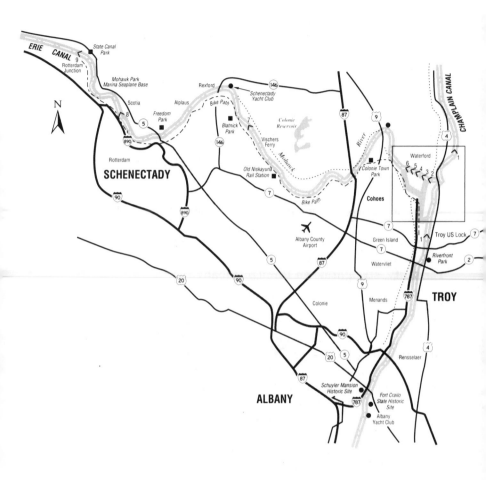

years of awful pollution. Now there is a new river front park with a boat launch, the Corning Preserve, just south of the railroad bridge. Albany Yacht Club, on the eastern side of the river in Rensellaer, is your best tie-up. Once north of the Port, most of the river traffic you'll encounter are rowers, a sport going through its own renaissance. The city does not present a welcoming countenance from the river. Intentional or not, the expressway builders very effectively separated the people from the river. That's changing due to a thoughtful and more enlightened outlook on the part of the city's administration and citizenry...but massive piles of concrete are hard to work around, even harder to humanize.

This was a major staging area in the French and Indian War. During the Revolution, the main element of British strategy was to separate feisty New England from the other (perhaps less committed?) colonies by driving a wedge from Montreal to New York City, straight down through Albany.

Practically all of the old downtowns of the cities comprising the capital district have been rebuilt. Albany's revival, fittingly enough, gained impetus from the futuristic Governor Nelson A. Rockefeller Empire State Plaza, a collection of new state buildings and older offices. Some people have visceral, outspoken opinions about the architecture and design of the Plaza. Be sure to visit it. It's also called THE MALL, and it's not like any mall you are familiar with. To some, it may be striking--it's certainly imposing, there is a beauty here--but it is definitely not warm and human.

You'll see the tallest buildings of the Plaza long before you reach Albany--whether you come by car, train, bike or boat. The New York State Museum--one of the architecturally distinct buildings on the mall--has permanent and changing exhibits that have always been worth-while. For years it had just kept getting better but now they are literally passing the hat. There are a lot of great museums in the State and--even including New York City's--this is right at the top. Founded in 1836, it is the oldest and largest state museum in the country and is a leading research and educational institution in geology, biology, anthropology and history. Allow at least a half-day. (518) 474-5843.

There's another museum in the Education Building, across Washington Street, with some fine Indian and geologic collections. Go to the observation deck on the 42nd floor of the Corning Tower, where on a clear day you can almost see the entire Northeast. You'll certainly see the Adirondacks to the north, the Greens of Vermont and the Berkshires of western Massachussets. To the south there are the rugged Catskills and the gentler

The State Capitol is also an educational and cultural center.

Helderbergs, all with a beauty of their own. Go see the State Capitol, the legislative chambers--especially the Senate, and the eye-popping Performing Arts Center, otherwise known as the "egg". There are many really good special programs and performances at the "egg"--another architectural landmark-- but check the schedule well in advance. Tickets are only sold direct, not through agencies. Ask to be put on their mailing list. Call or write to the Empire State Performing Arts Center, P. O. Box 2065, Albany, NY 12220. (518) 473-1845.

Underlying the Mall is an all-weather enclosed concourse connecting state office buildings, the egg, garages, tower, legislature, and museum. It's notable for scope, scale, shops, restaurants, and an amazing art collection that Governor Rockefeller had the state buy to decorate his monument.

The ugliest building in town is the close-by Governor's Executive Mansion. And it also has an outstanding art collection. (518) 474-2418

There are, however, some outstanding colonial mansions and homes: The Schuyler Mansion State Historic Site (518) 474-3953; Cherry Hill (518) 434-4791; and the Ten Broeck Mansion (518) 436-9826). Downtown Albany is fun to walk around. There are a lot of good restaurants but my all-time favorite is Jack's Oyster House at the bottom of State Street almost to Broadway. (518) 465-8854. Washington Park--a serene urban setting--is a few blocks west of the Plaza. Walk through the park, around the lagoon and along the bordering streets with their meticulously restored and maintained town houses dating from the mid-to late-1800's. Another personal favorite: The Albany Institute of History and Art. Usually referred to as a regional musuem, it is really much more. An Egyptian collection--complete with two mummies--is not what one would expect to find in a "regional" museum. There is a lot of specifically regional importance here but the art collections are a pre-cursor and a respectable sample of national art. The Hudson River School, because of what the movement came to represent in America and where it took place, is exceptionally well-represented through all of its phases. Closed Mondays. (518) 463-4478.

Before you leave Albany, walk over to Robinson's Square,

34

an attractive area of small shops, boutiques, and authentic possibilities for good dining.

Heading up the river, that's Watervliet (referred to as West Troy in old accounts of the canal) to port and Troy to starboard.

Watervliet has a rich history in the early days of the canal. It was really the beginning, or end, of the canal trip itself. Rafts of barges were assembled or disassembled here for the river trips to New York City. The cultural life of the town was expressly designed to separate canallers from their money. It was a colorful, rough town of saloons, gambling and bawdy houses. catering to a rough crowd with pockets full of wages from having just completed a run down the canal. Watervliet's main industry today is a U. S. Army Arsenal. Established in 1813, this is where the really BIG guns are made.

If you haven't been to Troy in a while, you should see her now. Always an eminently walkable city, it is now even nicer. Friendly, warm, welcoming and the Town Docks are right in town! This is the last opportunity to have your mast hauled before entering the lower clearances of the canal. The public docks are located literally under and just north of the Green Island Lift Bridge. Although there has been some actual real reconstruction, demolishing of collapsed areas, and new building, most of Troy's re-birth has been more of the clean-up, fix-up, spruce-up variety. There are some fine restaurants here--Italia, LoPorto's, Verdile's and the newer Zoleo among the Italian ones. The Castaways is located overlooking the docks.

Some of America's finest educational achievements occurred in Troy. Liberal education for women was introduced here by Emma Willard. The School bearing her name is a proud living monument to her and today is the oldest boarding and day school for young women in the country. While "girls" schools all over the country were turning coed, Emma Willard steadfastly remained single-sex.

Those impressive buildings high on the bluff above Troy are part of Rensellaer Polytechnic Institute, one of the country's premiere science and engineering schools. Tours daily throughout the year. (518) 276-4636.

THE NEW ERIE CANAL

Water coursing into Troy and its surroundings from the hilly plateau to the east made this an important industrial center early in the nineteenth century. If you are interested in industrial archaelogy, tours are arranged by Hudson-Mohawk Industrial Gateway, itself headquarted in a nice piece of commercial archaelogy. They have a range of trips, tours and day cruises to interesting places in the Capital district and beyond. Some are real surprises. Reservations are needed. Write or call for a brochure. Hudson-Mohawk Industrial Gateway, Burden Iron Works Building, Foot of Polk St., Troy, NY 12180-5539. Phone: (518) 274-5267

Now Troy is aiming successfully at attracting high-tech industry with special inducements and ready access to Rensellaer Polytechnic Institute.

From downtown Troy it's only about a third of a mile to Lock 1, the only Federal dam and lock on the canals, and the end of tides. Stay well south of the dam to avoid turbulence when this high volume lock empties; also avoid the shallow western side. Pleasure boats are locked through on the hour so just sit tight and look for the green light. Besides, the waterfall off the Troy dam is really a pretty sight from downstream. There are transient docks at Trojan Marine less than a mile above Lock 1. Other facilities too--fresh water, fuel, pumpout, courtesy car.

A half-mile north, on the west shore, is Cohoes Boat Marina and Van Schaick Island Marina. It is an island but bridges cross directly into downtown Cohoes.

The city owes its origins to the existence of Cohoes Falls, abundant water power that operated an extensive complex of mills. Some of those same mills, old wooden floors swept and bricks painted, now house a collection of factory outlets and discount stores. Direct from the manufacturer outlet stores are the nineties latest retail rage but this small city started attracting them about two generations ago. Cohoes Manufacturing Company--the "anchor store" if this were a mall--long ago outgrew its old mill and is still expanding in a modern site. Despite its name, this is not a manufacturer. It's a huge retail clothing and accessories outlet for all kinds of name brands. A genuine cultural and architectural attraction across the street is the Cohoes Music

Hall. Built in 1874 on the third and fourth floors of a four-story office and retail building, this little theatre has been rightfully called a "gem". During its early years it was the center of the community's cultural life but a sagging roof truss closed it in 1905. Re-birth began in 1969 when a local bank gave the site to the city; by 1974 performances had again started and now local repertory companies and visiting troupes offer a rich bill of fare. 518-235-7969.

Cohoes Falls must be the original "thundering cataract". This was the first block to westward navigation. On the Mohawk just before it empties into the Hudson, it is a spectacular sight during the spring melt. In the late eighteenth and early nineteenth centuries, many who looked at these falls thought the idea of a canal around them foolhardy.

Unless it is late in the season or particularly dry, the Falls are worth a short trip up the hill. You can best appreciate their awesome power up close from a small overlook perched on the south bank. Follow Route 32 about 1/4 mile west from the world class shopping.

There are several more marinas in the short stretch up river from Cohoes. Whether you are going north on the Champlain (Chapter X) or west on the Erie, this is a good opportunity for water, fuel, stocking-up.

You can transit Lock 1, the Federal dam at Troy without lower vertical clearances but from this point on there are you need to be below 15-1/2 feet if you are going north up the Champlain. Travel the Erie west with up to 20 feet to Three Rivers Point at the junction with the Oswego Canal. On the Erie from there to Tonawanda outside Buffalo some bridges have 15-1/2 foot clearances. The Cayuga--Seneca Canal is also 15-1/2 feet; the Oswego Canal is 20 feet.

Leaving the Hudson just past the Fourth Street bridge, you'll begin the ascent of Locks 2 through 6. There is a Canal Park and long wall for tie-ups below Lock 2. The walk into Waterford is a short one but there aren't many real restaurants or stores on the main street. A short walk on the road to Cohoes will find fast food.

In under two miles you'll rise 165 feet. The flight of locks operate in succession; it takes about 1-1/2 to 2 hours to make the lift. If you miss a series, just tie up and wait! Extra crew have the option of walking up to a nicely situated Canal Park at Lock 6 where they'll find charcoal grills and picnic tables. (If you are making this passage from west to east, Light 5 marks the beginning of the flight down from Lock 6 to 2.)

Just out of Lock 6, you'll pass two guard gates. Continuing west keep red buoys to starboard, white to port. Remnants of an aqueduct where the original Erie crossed the Mohawk from a sidecut in the north bank can be seen at Crescent Bridge. There are five marinas in the next four-to-five miles along the north shore in this stretch of the river. A sidecut from the original Erie Canal, still filled with water, can be seen along the north shore. Seven miles out of Lock 6 and after passing the double span Northway Bridge, you'll come to Lock 7 on the South shore, with a lift of 27 feet. On the north bank, before you reach the lock, watch for the remaining abutment of an old ferry landing. (There is also a rusty "Pipe Crossing" sign.) You can put ashore here to visit the historic village of Vischer's Ferry. From the old landing, it is only a short walk to the village, a charming collection of Greek Rivival homes dating from the early 1800's. There are no stores, but if you turn left at the intersection, there is a good apple farm with seasonal produce about a half mile to the west. It's a fairly good bike ride--but scenically rewarding--to shopping centers. There are also several good farmstands on north shore back roads--and a good one is straight north on Vischer Ferry Road.

A Coast Guard Auxiliary station is located just above Lock 7 with tie-ups and anchorage. The Hudson-Mohawk Bikeway passes through here. There are no stores within easy riding distance of the lock but it's great biking in either direction.

This broad sweeping loop of the river around the Capital District sees a lot of water and bicycle-borne recreational activity. There are parks, marinas, boat launching sites, rowing clubs, game preserves, historic districts, racing canoes and shells, and fishing. Especially, don't forget the fishing.

Since the river's clean-up a few years ago, the Mohawk has become a potent bass fishery. The water doesn't have a crystal-clear clean look so it somewhat belies being called a "clean" river. A slight muddy-murkiness is caused by colloidal clay in suspension. The river has probably looked something like this since the glaciers left about 12,000 years ago. Bass seem to like it, and I've seen bodacious walleyes pulled from these waters. Some fishing areas of the Mohawk are actually what the outdoor magazines would call "hot spots."

The Schenectady Yacht Club, about 4.5 miles west of Lock 7 on the north shore right at the Rexford Bridge, has some transient tie-ups and is good dockage while visiting the city. The only problem is that the SYC is not in Schenectady. There is an anchorage on the south shore, a few feet west of the bridge by the rowing and canoe dock, and some informal slips. Parts of the Erie Canal Aqueduct that crossed the Mohawk here still stand, wedged between the yacht club and the bridge. There is a small grocery store about a four minute walk from the yacht club in Rexford. Shopping is about two miles south on Route 146 (Balltown Road). Or, you can pick up the bicycle path on

The quaint hamlet of Vischer's Ferry has changed little since the the Greek revival homes were built in the early 1800's.

the south shore for a straight and easy--but not too pretty--ride into downtown Schenectady. Also on the north shore, about a mile west of the Schenectady Yacht Club and just beyond the mouth of Alplaus Kill (great bass spot), is the Mohawk Park Marina and Seaplane Base. This is a good spot for extended tie-ups. The little store in the village of Alplaus-- "place of eels" in old Dutch--has cold cuts and convenience items; there is fresh produce at the end of the road from the marina. Two miles along on the river there's a friendly old tavern, with a few tie-ups hard by the new Freeman's Bridge. The Western Gateway Bridge between Schenectady and Scotia is 11 minutes away. This is the area closest to downtown but there are no tie-ups.

Dutch traders and settlers started coming into this part of the wilderness in the 1620's. Plainly visible from the river, the Stockade on the south shore and east of the highway bridge is Schenectady's original settlement. It was founded in 1661 and early on was a rival trading center to Albany, then Beverwyck. There were 400 residents and 60 houses in the Stockade when 114 French and 96 Indians from Canada raided and burned the frontier outpost in February 1690, killing 60, taking 27 captive, and leaving the survivors to die in the cold without shelter. After the massacre, the good folks of Beverwyck decided that it might be prudent to keep the outpost as a buffer against repeated hostile incursions; the rivalry between the settlements cooled.

Much of the Stockade is still standing today in beautiful condition, a living collection of functioning colonial homes meticulously maintained by individual owners. For information call 518-393-8622 or 518-393-3290.

That distinguished-looking colonial house on the (west) Scotia side of the bridge was the manor house of a Scots trader for the Dutch West India Company. The first house on this site-- but closer to the river--was built in 1658. The present structure dates from the early 1700's. The house stayed in the Glen family until 1961. It is now a restaurant and available for banquets, parties, corporate functions, receptions. Guided river cruises leave daily from the Mansion's dock during the season. It's an interesting place to visit--for history and the architectural content of an early colonial house. (518) 374-7262. Collins Park (Freedom

Park) is across the highway, a pleasant place with swimming pond, picnic area and more Little League games than you can keep track of. A history of the area is recreated in a series of small kiosks, erected during the Bicentennial, along the river. There is a small boat ramp and a canoe dock but with so many interesting places to visit it's a pity there are no slips for visiting yachtsmen. You can anchor north of Cayuga Island but the highway bridge has too much traffic to make it a comfortable overnight.

The Schenectady County Historical Society is appropriately housed in a prime example of colonial architecture.

For many years, Schenectady was a General Electric "company town"; GE employment is now a mere shadow of what it was.

Passengers on the packet boats usually skipped this time-consuming section of the water-borne journey from Waterford by an overland trip of only three hours from Albany. Indeed, passenger traffic was so great between Albany and Schenectady that America's first inter-city railroad--a passenger only line--was started here in 1831, only five years after the canal opened. Lock 8 (south shore) is about 2.5 miles beyond the bridge and already the view from the river is more rural.

Another five miles brings you to Rotterdam Junction and Lock 9. During World War II there were two major military staging sites here--at the Scotia Naval Depot and the Army's Rotterdam facility. Trains streamed in from the west. Reassembled, they headed out to the ports around New Jersey, New York City, Boston and Canada. In those days of coal-burning steam locomotives, so much traffic went through here that the sky stayed dark. It is still an important rail junction.

There is a canal park in Rotterdam Junction and a short walk over the bridge at the lock brings you to a gro-cery/convenience store (ice too). Outstanding bass fishing below the dam.

As you move west from Lock 9, the view from the river brings the surrounding hills closer, and you push on into the Valley of the Mohawk.

BICYCLING

You could spend a week bicycling the Hudson--Mohawk Bikeway system running from downtown Albany to Rotterdam Junction, and linking up with all kinds of interesting places along the way. There are connections to other bicycle trails and to designated bikeways along local streets. The Bikepath so closely parallels the boating route that you can combine biking and boating for crew members who would rather pedal for a spell. Start the Bikeway in downtown Albany at the Erastus Corning Riverfront Preserve (there is a connector to Rensselaer by sidewalk

Riverfront Preserve (there is a connector to Rensselaer by sidewalk (!) over the Dunn Memorial Bridge.) Traveling north to Watervliet on the west shore, it is about seven miles to the Green Island Bridge crossing over to Troy. The Trail includes historic Lansingburg and Knickbacker Park. You can complete this loop on the eastern side of the Hudson with about three options: return south via Troy city streets and back to the Bike Trail over the Menands Bridge, cross the Waterford Bridge and return with an optional side trip to Cohoes and then back south through Watervliet, or continue on west on the south bank of the Mohawk. A connector in Cohoes puts you on the Riverspark's Heritage Trail, one of the Urban Cultural Parks in New York highlighting meaningful natural and historic sites. (518) 237-7999

Because so many decent roads and city streets are also available for biking, variations on these routes are endless. If you continue on west through Cohoes, be sure to stop at the Cohoes Falls Overlook. Even if it's a dry summer, you'll get an idea of the power of the falls when in flood.

The Bikeway here is mostly the old railroad right-of-way. At the right time of day--I'm partial to evening--the scenery borders on spectacular. Unimpeded views of the river coax you west through the Town of Colonie. This is a great stretch for bird-watching too.

At Forts Ferry Road, almost two miles west of the Northway Bridge, there are two historic houses: the 1820's Shaker Miller's house and Cornileus Reynold's house, built around 1848. Another two miles brings you to the now-restored old Niskayuna train station on the port side. It's a small structure, and looks just like you would expect for an old-time train station! No more trains...but it is on the main line of the Capital District Bikeway. Pleasant picnic spot with access to the beach.

Lock 7 is 2.5 miles west--picnic site, phones, and interesting lock operations here with a lift of 27 feet. Another picnic site is 1.3 miles west in the Niskayuna Town Park where the Bikeway takes on an abrupt steep uphill. It's a damn shame the route couldn't have continued along the river here on a dramatic cliff-side. But the Bikepath leaves the river and the old railroad right-of-way because General Electric had two major

43

facilites here: the Knolls Atomic Power Laboratory, and Corporate Research and Development Center. General Electric's corporate paranoia bullied the bike path away off the old rail line so there would be nothing between their sites and the river. I know how nice it could have been because, when the bikepath discussion first began in the mid-seventies, I walked along the old railroad right-of-way by swinging out over the cliff to get under GE's serious-looking fence at the R & D Center. The weird part is that Knolls, where nuclear engines for submarines are designed and could justifiably claim security concerns, always had walking access on the rail right-of-way until administrative nerds from R & D got into the act. Getting around the fence was no big deal--I could see where kids had been doing it. At the end of my really nice walk, I couldn't get around the western fence so I walked up the hill and introduced myself to the slightly spluttering security police. (They expected something; my approach was from the wrong direction.) General Electric's bureaucratic solution that sent the bike path 'round robin's barn must have cost 20 times more than just running it along the river where it belongs.

After passing the buttoned-up General Electric sites you have to negotiate another steep downhill, to get back to the river, of course. At the bottom of the hill is a teeny picnic site and the remnants of the old Erie Canal Aqueduct crossing over the Mohawk at Rexford.

It's about three miles to a cutoff at the new Freeman's Bridge; cross over the Mohawk here and follow the alternate bike path to reach Collins (Freedom) Park. Or, you can continue on the Bike Path into downtown Schenectady, founded in 1661, one of America's oldest cities. Jay Street has a block of quaint shops; City Hall is to be admired for its architecture; the library is one of the best you'll find in a city this size. The wide street running through downtown was once the old Erie Canal. In the last rebuilding of the canal when it was moved to the river, this segment was filled-in and now lives on as Erie Boulevard. Old timers remember being happy to get rid of the canal running through town; apparently the quiet water was rather smelly in the summertime, a complaint shared by other canal cities to the west. Union College's campus evokes memories of the days "when

I was a young and tender fellow." It's where Barbara Streisand and Robert Redford filmed "The Way We Were." Union claims to be the oldest college in the United States, having been chartered 1n 1795. There are some good restaurants around here too but it's a changeable scene. Ask the natives. Like Italian?

The best touristing in Schenectady is in the Stockade. Visit the Schenectady County Historical Society (32 Washington Avenue, 12305), park your bike and start the walk-about. A "Guide to Historic Schenectady", listing the area's historic buildings, is available from the Society. There is too much to see from a bike. These lovely old colonial homes can best be appreciated by walking. The Bikepath proper continues west at the Community College (the by-pass to Collins (Freedom) Park rejoins here). It's almost three miles to Lock 8 and five miles beyond to the end of the Bikeway, where you can cross over to the canal park at Lock 9. Lock 8 is the first of several moveable dams. Supported by bridge-like steel-works, the dam permits ice flow in winter when it is raised.

THE NEW ERIE CANAL

Chapter V

Mohawk Valley Region: Erie Canal to Amsterdam and West, Little Falls, Utica, Rome, to Oneida Lake; Locks 10 to 22

Even before the canal made navigation easy, this was one of the most well-traveled routes in New York. It was an Indian thoroughfare long before the Europeans came. Following a steady sequence of native encampments, French Jesuits came this way in the mid-1600's.

Many of the Indian sites along the Mohawk were seasonal but used so regularly over hundreds of years that they were permanent in the native culture. One of the very favored places can be found in the flats just west of Scotia defined by a westerly-northwesterly-northerly bend in the river. This ancient Indian camping ground, now owned by a local stone and gravel company, is sort of an "open" archaelogical site and until just recently was a rich source of early pre-Iroquois artifacts. Another site on the Hudson, from the same time and culture and used also as a seasonal base, was thoroughly examined, documented and carried off to the Museum at the Education Building in Albany by State archaelogists, leaving this one surplus and more or less exposed to casual exploration. All you had to do was dig, but it's pretty well dug out by now.

Although the Dutch made Schenecady their frontier outpost in 1661, they continued to push right up this beautiful, yielding valley--first as traders and trappers and then as settlers.

The valley's strategic importance made it a linear skirmish ground during the French and Indian Wars. During the Revolution a major battle at Oriskany prevented British reinforcements from reaching Saratoga and giving to the United States the decisive victory that won the war.

Long before the canal was even discussed, there was a busy river traffic between Schenectady--the lower end of navigation--and Little Falls 56 miles to the west. Flat bottom

Mohawk Valley

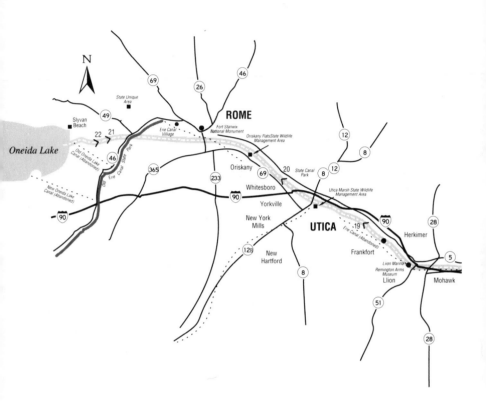

N

Oneida Lake

State Unique
Area

Slyvan
Beach

Old Oneida Lake
Canal (Abandoned)

New Oneida Lake
Canal (Abandoned)

Old Erie Canal State Park

Erie Canal
Village

ROME

Fort Stanwix
National Monument

Oriskany Flats State Wildlife
Management Area

Oriskany

State Canal
Park

Whitesboro

Yorkville

New York
Mills

New
Hartford

Utica Marsh State Wildlife
Management Area

UTICA

Frankfort

Erie Canal (Abandoned)

Llion Marina
Remington Arms
Museum

Llion

Herkimer

Mohawk

69
26
46
49
22
21
46
365
233
90
90
69
20
12
8
12
8
12
8
90
28
19
90
5
28
51
129
8

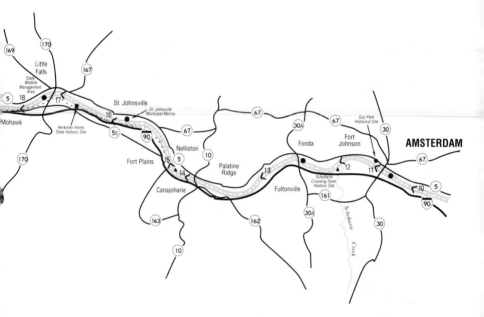

169 170

Little
Falls
State
Wildlife
Management
Area

167

5 18 17

Mohawk

Herkimer Home
State Historic Site

St. Johnsville

St. Johnsville
Municipal Marina

16

5S

90

67

67

Fonda

30A

67

Guy Park
Historical Site

30

Fort
Johnson

AMSTERDAM

67

170

Nelliston

10

5

Fort Plains

15

14

Canajoharie

13

Palatine
Ridge

Fultonville

161

Schoharie
Crossing State
Historic Site

12

11

10 5

90

163

162

30A

30

10

Schoharie Creek

LEGEND

Navigable Canal		Bike Path
Lock and Lock Number — symbol points to the higher canal elevation	26	Abandoned Canal
Terminal — docking only	●	City
Terminal — with park facilities	● Riverfront Park	Interstate Highway 90
Park	■ Colonie Town Park	Touring Route (U.S., State) or State Parkway 20 5
State Boat Launching Site	▲	

boats were poled upstream to the portage at Little Falls, where, according to a 1796 Report of the Directors of the Western Inland Lock Navigation Companies, a private company incorporated to improve western navigation, goods had to be hauled "over a road as rough, rocky and bad as the imagination can conceive."

Double-ended batteux, without a deck, about 30 by 5 feet and carrying about one-and-a-half tons of cargo were used on this section of the Mohawk from 1720 to 1825. Pushed along by 12 foot poles, sometimes by sail, (that must have been difficult-- I've tried sailing a canoe on the Mohawk) with a steering oar lashed to a sternpost and usually manned by a crew of three, these craft were said to have been portageable! Must have been a different breed of men. The larger Schenectady (Durham) boats, introduced in 1797 and lasting until 1825, were really the first canal boats. Usually with a crew of five, these sturdy craft could carry 12 tons and weighed about 10 tons--too much even for those iron men to portage--and were limited to the lower Mohawk between Schenectady and Little Falls. The vessel had wonderful antecedents: its flat-bottomed, straight-sided, 60 by 8 foot design copied Pennsylvania ore boats--the very same used by General Washington to attack Trenton. Its linear ancestors first tracked through England's narrow canals and later were well-documented in Canada working the St. Lawrence flow. They were equipped with oars, sails, tow ropes and 18 foot iron-tipped setting poles. Steering was accomplished by a long sweep hinged with an iron pin to a sternpost.

The foredeck on the Schenectady boats carried sail attached to a hinged mast so that it could be folded for passage under bridges. In those times farmers constructed private bridges to reach fields on opposite sides of the river. Most were inexpensively built, often jury-rigged, invariably low. When the Erie arrived these structures posed a real problem and the inspiration for that frequent cry made famous by song: Low bridge, everybody down!

Navigation was aided by V shaped dams constructed of rocks to help build a head of water. Aim the boat for the opening at the bottom of the V coming downstream--just exactly like white-water canoeing. Must have been fun...or hair-raising. Wonder

50

if any of those guys dumped? They must have. Upstream? A tougher problem calling for determined poling and tow ropes.

Overland transportation was so arduous in most places that the opportunity to float goods, even for a short stretch of travel, was very appealing.

Improvements to the Mohawk by the privately financed Western company by 1798 had already reduced the cost of shipping a ton from Albany to Seneca Lake from $100 to $32. Locks had been built around Little Falls where the river drops 39 feet in three-quarters of a mile; two locks west of Rome opened to Wood Creek. The new "Durham" or "Schenectady" boat, with its 60 foot length and 16 ton capacity was a giant leap forward over the one-and-a-half tons the 30 foot bateau could haul. The work of the Western company, perpetually short of funds and expertise, navigating only part of the year when there was abundant water, got no further than Oneida Lake. Nevertheless, the advantages of water-borne commerce began to have a profound effect on the citizenry.

There is no bad way to make this lovely trip up the Mohawk Valley. It is, of course, a lot of fun in a boat and my primary perspective in this chapter. But I don't mean to slight any other mode of travel. Even though the shoulders and berm are kind of skimpy in places, the generally light traffic and low-key villages make Route 5S decent bicycling. Route 5 is great too--and there are chances to cross back and forth at several spots.

Pedaling a leg of the Hudson-Mohawk Bikeway here from the Schenectady Community College to Lock 9 in Rotterdam Junction is a scenic and historically rich ride with several sections of the abandoned canal bordering the bike path.

The rail trip on Amtrak through the valley here is the prettiest section of the ride between Albany and Buffalo! Just get a seat on the left side of the car as it heads west.

Driving along the NYS Thruway is scenic in its own right and the only way to go if you have to be there now. But we're talking about doing things for fun: So drive along Route 5S one way and try Route 5 on the opposite shore another time. Take your time, walk around the little towns, buy fresh fruit and veggies at the farm stands.

51

THE NEW ERIE CANAL

It takes about 40 minutes to cruise from Lock 9 to Lock 10 where you'll find a 15 foot lift and fresh water just east of the lock. Look for parts of the original Erie along the river's south shore. Another three miles brings you to the Amsterdam terminal--tie-ups, fresh water, and access to the City of Amsterdam. At Lock 11 you'll also find tie-ups and anchorage.

At one time this was the "Rug City", named for all the carpet mills in town. It is hard to imagine that it was once a vibrant, busy city. By the turn of the century, a constant stream of immigrants--mostly middle European, German and Italian kept these mills humming. One of the biggest names in the industry--Mohawk Carpet Mills--was located here. Now, thanks to new technology, anybody with a mere quarter-of-a-million dollars for a carpet making machine can get into the business. It's great for us consumers but knocked the stuffing out of what once was a giant of American industry.

Most of Mohawk's old factory buildings continued standing as forlorn hulks until a mammoth fire recently wiped out even the standing reminders of a powerhouse of old American industry. A surprising number, however, had been sub-divided and were anonymously (or perhaps with a modest little sign) occupied by all kinds of businesses--packaging, electronics, distribution, assembly.

Like other cities further along the Mohawk, Amsterdam became an industrial power back in the days of water power. Powerful streams literally fall into the city--water power had to be used close to the source of mechanical conversion. There is one remarkably pretty stream roaring down right into downtown Amsterdam. Those cosy bluffs to starboard are actually the foothills of the Adirondacks. From here to Rome, you are never far from some pretty good trout fishing.

There is so little of the old downtown Amsterdam left that it's sad to even try to find it. But you will find a mall, close-by the river.

Natives like to tell you that the famous actor Kirk Douglas grew up in Amsterdam. I understand he has mixed feelings about his childhood here. Well, it's certainly easier for a Jewish kid to get a paper route today.

Ingenious restoration saved the historic Schoharie Creek Aqueduct.

There's a state historic site--one of the stately homes built by Sir William Johnson-- on the grounds of Lock 11 at Guy Park. Sir William was the most powerful white man in this area in pre-Revolutionary times. He traveled widely representing the British Crown and was enormously influential with the Indians. The house at Guy Park was built for his daughter and her husband, Guy Johnson.

About 12 minutes out of Lock 11 you can get another look at the walls of the original canal on the south shore. Lock 12 is almost five miles west of Lock 11, but halfway along you can visit Fort Johnson. Sir William built this in 1749. It's now the home and museum of the Montgomery County Historical Society. This period museum, open in the summer months, has some worth-while Indian collections.

Barely out of Fort Johnson there are some partially restored sections of the Old Erie and the remains of an original lock.

THE NEW ERIE CANAL

Five minutes beyond Lock 12 is the Schoharie Creek Historic Site where the Schoharie Creek enters the Mohawk. The Schoharie Valley to the south is a beautiful, beautiful place. By all the measurements of modern agriculture, it's a small area, not much larger than a couple of Nebraska wheat farms. But during Colonial days this was a major grain-growing area--the "Breadbasket of the Revolution." About a half mile up the creek, you can get a look at a remarkable piece of engineering constructed in the 1840's--the Schoharie Creek Aqueduct, 13 piers with 40 foot arches, a cut limestone structure that carried the first re-built canal over the creek. This section was troublesome-- maybe cursed--from the start. The original canal crossed the creek behind a dam here. Tricky and sometimes dangerous, barges were drawn across by windlasses. Many were swept away by swift current and smashed on the rocks below. One of the priorities in the first re-building was an improved passage through this scenic area. A century and a half later, piers supporting the NYS Thruway bridge here were undermined by creek scouring when a storm suddenly flooded the valley. The bridge collapse was instantaneous and catastropic. Motorists speeding through the mist plunged to their death on the rocks far below.

The aqueduct gained a fame of its own as a favorite artwork appearing on English china. Now, thanks to modern engineering you can see the main bulwarks of this classic structure today. The aqueduct started to fall apart several years ago; once an arched section collapsed, the adjoining sections caved in on it. The problem of restoration/preservation presented many challenges but elegant engineering solutions saved what's left. The real technical story is in what you can't see--the innovative solutions at work inside of the arches, explained in a series of plaques in the park at the anchorage in the mouth of the creek.

The Schoharie Creek looks like it might have trout potential. No trout in these lower reaches but it is a great small mouth bass fishery. Farther up the stream there are lots of very nice-to-look-at productive waters. Try a fly rod or light spin gear. These guys are not huge fish but they live in fast water and they do fight.

A few minutes of motoring (1.8 miles west of Buoy 247)

54

brings you to Auriesville, I guess you would call them the rosy beige buildings, on the hill to the south, kind of a distinctive landmark along the New York State Thruway. This is The Shrine of Our Lady of Martyrs, dedicated to the first North American saints. Here, in the Mohawk village of Osseruenon on October 18, 1646, the French Jesuit priest Father Isaac Jogues, was killed. The memorial is for him, two Brothers and five mission priests. Nearby is a grotto in memory of Kateri Tekakwitha, a Mohawk maiden who became the first American born saint.

Auriesville is only about a mile from the boat launch at Schoharie Crossing State Historic Site, an easy walk west on Route 5S. There are two very good produce stands along the way. Just past the second produce stand, a road leads to the East Parking Lot by the Coliseum Church--this saves a longer walk by way of the formal approach to the shrine further west. You can also reach the shrine from The Poplars Inn (marina, restaurant, motel) in Fultonville, Exit 28 of the NYS Thruway, about three miles west. The Poplars should be called "the popular" because in season this is a busy place, the most complete marina complex on the Erie. They even offer river cruises! (518)-853-4511.

Another 3.5 miles on the river from Schoharie Crossing brings you to the Fultonville Bridge and the Fonda terminal. That's Fultonville on the south and Fonda on the north. You can tie up on the Fonda side; restrooms and phone too. I don't know why they call it the Fultonville Bridge. Fonda is perhaps the more famous of the two towns. After all, it's where the famous Henry Fonda acting clan originated. The bridge must have been named before anyone ever figured out that Henry came from here. He really didn't like to acknowledge his New York roots. Jane has been more generous. Back in the Schenectady Stockade one of the older houses was a Fonda home and the old Dutch name keeps appearing in other places--there's a Fonda Road in the Town of Crescent.

If you would like to follow-up on Sir William Johnson, the home he built in 1763 is three miles north of Fonda in Johnstown. Now a state historic site, it has a good collection of antique furniture and some of Sir William's personal artifacts.

Another musuem worth visiting is the Mohawk--

THE NEW ERIE CANAL

Caughnawaga, at the site of the Kateri Tekakwitha memorial, a half mile west of Fonda on Route 5. Many Indian artifacts have been recovered from excavations here, the location of an extensive Indian village.

Lock 13, with a lift of 8 feet, is five miles west of the Fultonville Bridge. Then it's 2.5 miles to an anchorage by the "Noses", (look for Buoy 323). These rocky towers--654 and 414 feet above the river--were formed by the river working its way through a hard ridge. Indians made good use of these commanding sites.

Canajoharie is a busy little village on the south bank. Stock up on practically everything: ice, groceries, newspapers. There is a supermarket here. Small one, but a supermarket nonetheless. Tie-ups and anchorage at the Canajoharie Terminal-- 8.6 miles west of Lock 13. The historic Van Alstyne house in Canajoharie has a large collection relating to early Mohawk valley history. It's a distinctive one-and-a-half story building erected in 1749 by Marte Janse Van Alstyne. The Tryon County Committee on Safety--militia who fought under General Nicholas Herkimer in the important battle at Oriskany--was headquartered here in 1774-1775. George Washington visited on his 1783 trip through the region.

Wintergreen Park, in Canajoharie Gorge just south of the town, offers picnicking, camping and nature walks. The village got its name from the Indian expression for the gorge--"pot that washes itself."

Art lovers will be nicely surprised by the Library and Art Gallery. Gifts from one of the founders of Beech-Nut, Bartlett Arkell, made possible a meaningful selection of American works, including priceless Homers and some outstanding paintings of the original Erie. Usually open 'til 4:30, 9:30 on Thursday and 1:30 on Saturday. Closed Sunday. (518) 673-2314.

It's not quite a half-mile to Lock 14--lift of 8 feet-- from the Canajoharie Terminal (7.9 miles from Lock 13.) Tie-ups above the lock, and a park on the island. The river and its locks dominate the narrow valley--whether you are traveling by auto, boat, rail or bicycle. The New York State Thruway, village, and Route 5S hug the south bank, the railroad and Route 5 a stone's throw to the north.

The Fort Plain bridge is about one-half mile before Lock 15. There's another 8 foot lift at Lock 15, almost four miles west. This is the last of the movable dams--or the first if you're coming from the west. About a third of a mile past the lock, at Buoy 383, the Fort Plain Museum off Route 5S marks the site of a Revolutionary War fort. Colonial and Indian artifacts. A municipal marina at St. Johnsville, 6.2 miles past the Lock 15, just before the bridge to starboard, has launching ramp, gas and diesel, ice, phone and showers. In the Margaret Reaney Memorial Library at 19 Kingsbury Avenue, you'll find an interesting array of china, glass, bronzes, military buttons, Indian artifacts, paintings and geneological records. Open afternoons.

Approaching Lock 16 (1.8 miles beyond the St. Johnsville Marina) you can see parts of the Old Erie along the south bank. There's a 20.5 feet lift; anchorage near old dam; tie-ups above the lock. An old canal tavern is west of the lock. The Barge Inn, food and cocktails, is only a few minutes walk.

Parenthetical note for trout fishermen: North of here beyond Route 29 and generally between the crossroads of Lassellsville, Dolgeville and Oppenheim there used to be some outstanding trout fishing in the Sprite and Middle Sprite. Also in East Canada Creek. I say "used to" because I haven't been there lately. These streams come out of the Adirondacks and acid rain has treated the area shamefully. The Sprites are woodsy small to mid-size streams, just delightful, tricky for fly fishing but great fun for ultra-light spinning. Canada Creek is wide-open riffles, designed for fly fishing.

Even if you don't fish, this is a great area to explore because the countryside has changed so much over the last 50 years. Buy the Lasselsville quadrangle topographic map because it is such a gem of an historical curiosity. None of the back roads go where they are supposed to. Farms, fences and any sensible landmarks have disappeared along with the people who abandoned this marginal soil.

Indian Castle Church, about a half mile past Lock 16, gets its name from one of the old Indian fortified sites, called Indian Castles." Between 1700 and 1775 this was the upper

General Nicholas Herkimer's homestead is rich in the history of colonial America and of Palitinate Germans.

castle of the Mohawk Bear Clan. In 1756 Sir William Johnson built Fort Hendrick here, named for the Indian, King Hendrick, who had been killed the year before in the battle at Fort William Henry, now Lake George village. Daniel Muller, under commission by Sir William, built the church in 1769.

Just before reaching Mindenville Bridge, a half mile from Lock 16, there are remnants of Old Erie on the north bank. High Bridge comes up in a mile, followed by the Nowadaga Creek Guard Gate in 2.3 miles. the Lansings Street Bridge in just under a half mile and, finally, the Mohawk River Outlet and Dam in the next half mile. The dug canal becomes a river again.

Try to stop at the Herkimer Homestead. A 60 foot obelisk erected in honor of General Nicholas Herkimer can almost be seen from Buoy 457. This is not a high visibility tourist destination, but it should have more recognition because of the significance of General Herkimer's victory at the Battle of Oriskany. Like so many other attractive places that are tantalizingly close to the river, no direct access is provided for the boater. It is only a short walk or an easy bicycle ride from Lock 17. There is a collection of early furniture and artifacts from the colonial period and the Revolutionary War. It was built in 1764. A nice river setting, the General must have loved this place. One of the most interesting features of the audio-visual presentation at the Visitor Center next to the homestead is the history of the refugees from the German Palatinate who came to this country in the early 1700's. It is easy to reach the Herkimer Homestead from Exit 29A on the NYS Thruway--about a five minute drive. (315) 823-0398

A mile before Lock 17 you'll pass under Finck's Basin Bridge. The lock is 9.2 miles from Lock 16. At 40.5 feet, this is the highest lift lock of its type in the world! The vertical lift gates, much more common in Europe, are rarely seen in this country. For the uninitiated in locking through, this should probably not be the first lock entered. Looking straight up at 40 feet can be a little unsettling for some folks. Just remember sound boating practice and enjoy the vertical ride. Small craft should keep to the south wall on the lift. For such a large chamber, this one fills and empties amazingly fast, in about seven or eight minutes. There are tie-ups down river on the south wall. The Little Falls Terminal is 1.2 miles upstream from Lock 17, past the guard gate at the land cut, and under the Arterial bridge. Make fast here to visit the village.

Little Falls is an enjoyable small city or big village. There are good newsstands in town, some fine coffee shops and restaurants. It is a nice place to walk around; you should be able to find just about any provisions you might need. Years ago, when Schenectady was the lower limit of navigation by canoe and bateau, this was the upper limit. It was a difficult portage. Walk over to see the untamed sections of the river and you'll understand why. This was also the first section that Western Inland Lock Navigation tried to improve in the first attempt at building a canal in the 1790's. When the Erie arrived, an impressive 1184 foot arched stone aqueduct carried feeder water from the Mohawk here and served as a direct branch into the village.

Continuing to climb uphill, Lock 18 has a 20 foot lift, 3.7 miles west of the Little Falls Terminal. The canal leaves the river just before reaching the lock. Some anchorage in the outlet. There is also anchorage about a mile west of the Lock, along the south shore, and east of Light 506.

Now we're approaching an attractive sequence of Mohawk Valley towns: Herkimer, Mohawk and Ilion.

Two miles east from the town of Mohawk, on Route 5S, is the historic Fort Herkimer Church. During the French and Indian Wars, it was used as a fort. The church, built in 1737, had fallen into days of declining membership and disrepair when

Exiting Lock E-17 at Little Falls after dropping 40 feet!

it was bought and restored by the Reformed Church of America's Classis of Montgomery. Although the church is not open for visitors, it has become a favorite for weddings.

There's an anchorage 2.9 miles west of Lock 18, east of Light 507, along the south shore. But being so close to the Thruway it is rather noisy. Then, in close succession, you pass the Washington St. bridge, a Thruway bridge, the Mohawk guard gate, and the Mohawk St. bridge where you'll find the Herkimer Terminal. A fairly easy walk, or a very easy bicycle ride, takes you into town. Walking around, you can see that this was once a bustling, busy place. Like so many other old industrial cities, Herkimer peaked and declined. But Herkimer has made a nice comeback and is a pleasant place. The old downtown section from early in this century is not shabby but has a quaintness of its own.

From the Herkimer terminal, it is 1.8 miles to the Ilion Marina. 315-894-9758. There's a pumpout, ice, launch ramp, picnic tables, gas and diesel, fresh water, phone, electricity. Close-by is a motel, a really good restaurant and groceries. A great place to visit and only a short walk is the Remington Arms Museum, with its outstanding collection of firearms, everything from the flintlock to modern day weapons. If you are interested in guns, particularly sporting arms, this is a great place. But if anybody in your party is so inclined, go along, because the historical aspects are intriguing. In other words, you don't have to be interested in guns to enjoy and learn from the Remington Museum. You can spend three-quarters of an hour in here or hours, depending on how much you want know about some of the displayed firearms. There is a short movie; admission is free. During the summer months, it is open from 8 to 5 weekdays, and Saturday and Sunday afternoons. (315) 894-9961. The last time I was there, Remington even had a banner flying at the dock welcoming boaters! Immediately after leaving the marina, you'll pass under the Ilion bridge. The Frankfort terminal is 2.8 miles from the marina, about .4 of a mile after passing under the Frankfort bridge. The terminal is located in the river outlet; tie-ups and anchorage.

Lock 19 is four miles upstream from the Frankfort

The remains of old lock works can be visited a few yards east of the modern Lock E-17.

terminal. The lift is 21 feet. Another 7.8 miles brings you to the Utica Harbor lock (6.5 foot lift) with access to the State dock and Utica terminal. Fresh water and tie-ups. If you're planning to visit Utica--the largest city since Schenectady--you can tie-up here, if you don't mind the gritty industrial marine ambiance and a queasy feeling about leaving an unattended boat. Otherwise, drive on to the Marcy Marina.

Always an important industrial city, Utica has had its own renaissance. Its downtown--no different than many others in industrial America--fell into a funk as the suburban malls lured consumers from downtown. The city, however, has recovered a measure of its old vigor and is now a vital, interesting place. There are several outstanding restaurants, a modern hotel and many chic shops.

The tour of the Utica Club Brewery --formerly the West End Brewing Company, now the F. X. Matt Brewing Co.--is highly recommended. It includes a trolley ride, and only takes a little over a half hour. I was always a little confused about this brewery's name and just what brews it brewed. But the story is really straight-forward. The company was started in 1888 as the West End Brewing Company. During Prohibition it bottled near beer and sodas marketed as Utica Club, and, after repeal it was easier to get back into the beer business as Utica Club. And that became their big seller. For many years I enjoyed a superior brew called Matt's and thought it came from a small Utica brew-house. But my usual came from the big brewery in town; it was Matt's because he owned the whole place. And he has all along. F. X. is the grandson of the founder and just recently got around to putting the family name on the business. As interesting as all that is, I'm most intrigued by the fact that the F. X. Matt Brewing Company is the largest contract brewer in the United States! If you are a fan of local brews from almost anywhere around the country, chances are that your usual comes from here, not from the micro-brewer. Court and Varick Sts. Phone: (315) 732-0022

The Munson-Williams-Proctor Institute has an admirable collection of American and European paintings, graphic and decorative arts, and sculpture. 310 Genesee St. Phone: (315) 797-0000.

The Marcy Marina (315) 736-7617) is 2.4 miles from the Utica Lock. Close to groceries, it has electricity, gas, water, pumpout, hoist, showers. This is the most popular tie-up spot to visit Utica.

Lock 20 is only 1.5 miles west, where you'll find a delightful little park maintained by the Loyal Order of Moose. The fishing is what you would call "pretty good" with a little bit of everything and an occasional trout. Picnicking, rest rooms, pumpout. It is a 16 foot lift; groceries nearby. Lock 20 is the last "up" lock on the eastern section of the canal. You are now on a height of land, the "Rome Summit Level," the first completed segment of the Erie. In December 1818, eight years before the completion of the entire canal, water was let into a section three-quarters of a mile west of Rome. By 1820 the trial-and-error, experimental phase of canal building was over: navigation was being conducted 94 miles westward from Utica to the Seneca

River. Journals of the day recounted these events in emotionally charged articles. These were times of high spirits; canal fever reigned.

Halfway between Oriskany and Rome on Route 69, the Oriskany Battlefield is marked by a tall shaft with a descriptive plaque, describing this fight as the "turning point of the Revolution." General Nicholas Herkimer and a force of 800 Tryon Militiamen on their way to reinforce Fort Schuyler (Fort Stanwix) fell into a British trap here and fought one of the bloodiest battles of the war. General Herkimer was seriously wounded in the leg early in the fight. Lighting a pipe, he directed his troops while propped in his saddle against a tree. The Americans, in one of the bloodiest battles of the Revolution, held their own against General (some accounts call him Colonel) Barry St. Leger's Tories and Indians. I have heard the Battle of Oriskany described as an American defeat and, by equally competent historians, as a standoff. I'll go with the standoff version, because we did eventually win by holding fast. St. Leger's forces withdrew from

The pleasant small park at Lock E-20 gives picnickers a close-up view of locking operations.

the field. A few weeks later, he also withdrew from Fort Stanwix after we grittily outlasted the seige. Our stubborness--and at times that's all we had going for us--prevented British reinforcements from reaching the Hudson River Valley and made possible our victory at Saratoga that proved so decisive in winning Independence. Audio-visual presentation at the Visitor Center: (315) 768-7224. Also, Battle of Oriskany Historical Society Museum dioramas. Unfortunately, the battleground is another of those great places that is close to the canal but is difficult for boaters to reach. You can pick it right off on Chart 14786-E21. (The Marine charts are inconsistent about noting historic sites.) There is no direct land access from the canal although its straight-line distance is only a little more than a mile. If you do attempt to bike it, Lock 20 is the best place to tie-up. Anchoring by the bridge going into the village of Oriskany would get you 2.3 miles closer with about another 3.5 to go. Narrow shoulders and an almost bermless road make for difficult bicycling--but at least there aren't many big trucks. You don't overtly learn a lot by visiting the Battle Monument but you can get a feel for the lay of the land and understand how an ambush would have been very feasible. This is hallowed ground. You visit to pay your respects.

You can walk into downtown Rome from the Rome Terminal, 11 miles west of Lock 20. Try to arrive around dinnertime and try the Savoy, a favorite for so long that it's almost a Roman legend. Italian, of course.

Rome as a destination is fine in itself. But don't leave town without seeing the restoration at the site of Fort Stanwix. Indeed, the restoration is hard to miss, taking up an entire downtown city block. Brigadier General John Stanwix built the original fort in 1758 to protect the important portage between the Mohawk River and Wood Creek during the French and Indian Wars. Still strategically vital in the Revolution, the site guarded the main route from Canada to the Hudson River and the Eastern Seaboard. It was renamed Fort Schuyler in 1776 and manned by 550 Continentals under Colonel Peter Gansevoort. A British force of 1,400 Tories, Indians and Hessians laid seige to the fort for three weeks in August 1777. The Continentals were hard-pressed, always low on food and ammunition. Colonel Gansevoort carefully husbanded what resources he had and doggedly held on. General Nicholas Herkimer was on his way to relieve the fort when he was ambushed at what became the Battle of Oriskany. Benedict Arnold played a key role in defending Fort Stanwix too, leading a small band of reinforcements from Saratoga that the British had been deceived into thinking was much larger. When St. Leger learned of Arnold's advance, he lifted the siege and withdrew to Canada. Local lore claims that the Stars and Stripes--sewn from

The Oriskany Monument marks a critical, bloody Revolutionary battle.

a Continental soldier's white shirt, a ladies red petticoat and the blue coat of an officer-- first flew in battle here. You'll learn a lot about the battles, the daily life of Continental soldiers, and contemporary fortifications. Operated by the National Park Service, Fort Stanwix is open from April to December. Phone: (315) 336-2090

On July 4, 1817, construction of the original Erie started at what is now called Erie Canal Village, operated by the City of Rome. An 1840's canal village has been faithfully reconstructed here. Many attractions, including rides in a replica of a passenger packet in a section of the original canal, restored buildings, and a museum of the political, social and economic significance of the canal. It is four or five miles from the city not accessible on today's canal. Bicycle? yes, but along a very busy road; taxi? OK; walk? too far and not a pleasant walk.

This may be the best of all the canal museums but it runs on a weirdly truncated season--closing on Labor Day! Phone:

(315) 337-3999.

The Old Erie Canal State Park, one of the newest state parks, is a linear strip along the original canal and towpath, starting at the Erie Canal Village and continuing on to DeWitt, about 30 miles to the southwest in suburban Syracuse. The Syracuse end of the park is also not conveniently accessible from today's waterway. Following the perfectly flat old towpath, this is supposed to be a "bike and hike" trail. It's fine for walking but the bike path is mostly gravel and not really suitable for a road or touring machine. A mountain or one of the new "cross" bikes would do fine. One of the linear park's nicest features is direct access to Green Lakes State Park along the right-of-way. Green Lakes is a lovely, woodsy, place of rolling hills with a beautiful swimming lake, rowboat rentals, beach, picnic sites and a scenic, hilly golf course. A Canal Education Center, at the end of the Park in DeWitt, is operated under the direction of

Fort Stanwix, a critical site in both the French & Indian War and the Revolution, is right in the middle of Rome.

the Erie Canal Museum of Syracuse. Information from NYS Parks and Recreation, Central Region: Clark Reservation, Jamesville, N. Y. 13078 (315) 492-1756.

One of the longer-lasting lateral canals connected in Rome: The Black River Canal ran almost straight north along the flank of the Tug Hill Plateau for about 90 miles,eventually reaching Carthage. It was started in 1837, not completed until 1851, and amazingly endured until 1922 before it was abandoned. Many sections of the Black River Canal still survive.

A fine adventure is to drive from Rome up Route 46 and beyond looking for the silent history waiting along the roadside. The farther north you go, the better it gets. Take a camera. Who knows when you'll be back this way again.

Lock 21--your first "down" lock all the way from Waterford--is 7.6 miles from the Rome Terminal; lift of 25 feet. About two miles east of the lock you'll pass the New London Dry Dock, a commercial facility operated by the State. Lock 22--the last lock in this section of the canal--comes up in 1.6 miles. It has a lift of 25.1 feet. You are now at the level of Oneida Lake-- 369.9 feet above sea level-- a major recreational resource in this part of the country. There's a thriving summer colony here, attracted to this large inland lake and good--sometimes great-- fishing. As transportation has improved over the years, more summer cottages have been winterized and are now year-round homes. Full service marinas abound. There are seven facilities before you leave the canal for the lake. My last count found over 30 marinas around the lake with a widely varying range of amenities. Several of these marinas have launch ramps and campgrounds. You are never far from dockage and access to supplies.

Verona Beach State Park is a mile south of Sylvan Beach after exiting the canal. There are tie-ups at the Sylvan Beach Terminal, just east of the Sylvan Beach Bridge, and there are many commercial facilities in the immediate area. Some are campgrounds for family campers that have shoreline property and have added moorings for boaters. Practically all sell bait. Remember, this is a *good* fishing lake. Although there are a lot of marine facilities, most cater more to the fishing public than strictly serving the needs of boaters passing through.

Villages are located on both north and south shores. The Thruway is south, so there is more "civilization" down that way. Oneida, a little over seven miles south on Route 316 from the southeast corner of the lake, is known as the home of one of the more famous social experiments in utopian communal living in the mid 1800's. Today it is mostly visited to shop the Oneida Ltd. Silversmiths factory store (315) 361-3661. The biggest bargains are the "seconds". I can never see what's wrong with a piece unless it's pointed out to me.

The channel runs right through the middle of the lake. A 21 mile crossing into the prevailing westerlies suggests attention to the weather forecast. Charts are advisable...shallows on both the north and south shorelines. Buoys, indicated as white on Charts 14786-E-15, 16, and 17 are now green. The state maintains two hard surface launch ramps on the south shore, east of Bridgeport, on Route 31. If you're in the mood for a swim, head for the beautiful beach at Oneida Shores Park, just east of Brewerton. Really nice place for picnicking too.

There are several full-service marinas at Brewerton, as you return into the canal, and some fine, year-round restaurants. The Chamber of Commerce has a directory of services for boaters, color-keyed for walking distances and with phone numbers, on the north side of the second bridge coming in from the lake--by the dock next to the Waterfront Restaurant and Tavern. (The first bridge is the interstate.)

69

THE NEW ERIE CANAL

Chapter VI

Central Region: Erie Canal, Oneida Lake to Macedon, Syracuse; Montezuma National Wildlife Refuge; Locks 23 to 30

Returning to the canal at the western end of Oneida Lake means entering the Oneida River at Brewerton. The Oneida soon joins the eastward flowing Seneca River to form the Oswego River at Three Rivers Point. That's your route--a short fast-dropping run north--if you're headed for Lake Ontario. The main Erie pushes west on the Seneca River, branching off to Onondaga Lake to call on Syracuse, or dropping down into the Cayuga--Seneca Canal for the Finger Lakes.

Central New York is the only part of the state that is unambiguous about being "Upstate". People living in and around New York City consider themselves New Yorkers--authentic downstaters; to them everything north of Westchester is "upstate." In the Capital District--around Albany and Schenectady--they like to say they are living in Northeast New York. People in Binghamton, Elmira and Corning belong to the Southern Tier. Residents in the Catskills or Adirondacks, of course, live in "the mountains". Rochesterites don't mind being upstate, but Buffalo--really a mid-western city--is definitively western New York. Buffalo may belong to the "rust-belt", but because of the canal it is historically connected to the east, unlike other mid-west cities.

Syracuse is the capital of upstate New York.

Before the Oneida River channel was improved for navigation, shallow water made the site of Brewerton an easy ford. The good crossing and abundant fish made this site important to the Indians hundreds of years before the Europeans came. Many relics and artifacts of their civilization have been found along the banks. Samuel de Champlain came through here in 1615 with Huron braves and French soldiers. The missionaries didn't arrive until 1651. Settlement began in 1789, mostly as

71

Central Region

Lake Ontario

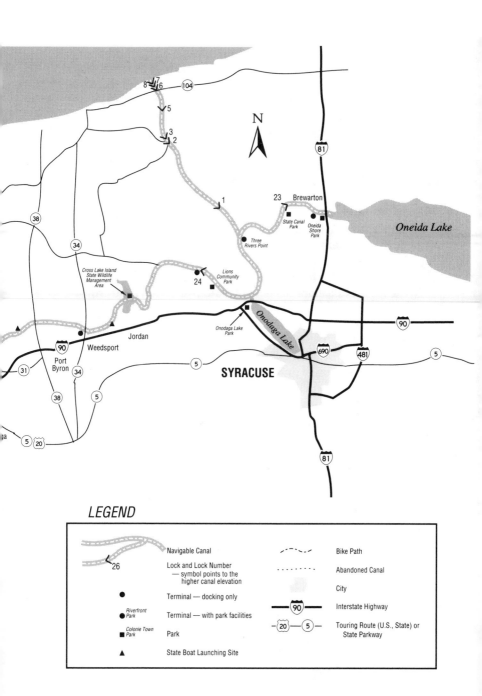

N

104

81

8 7 6
5
3
2
1

23 Brewarton
State Canal Park
Oneida Shore Park

Oneida Lake

Three Rivers Point

Cross Lake Island State Wildlife Management Area

Lions Community Park
24

Onodaga Lake

90

Onodaga Lake Park

38
34

Jordan

Weedsport

Port Byron

31
34
38
5

90

5

690
481
5

SYRACUSE

81

5 20

LEGEND

Navigable Canal	Bike Path
Lock and Lock Number — symbol points to the higher canal elevation	Abandoned Canal
26	
Terminal — docking only	City
Riverfront Park — Terminal — with park facilities	Interstate Highway 90
Colonie Town Park — Park	Touring Route (U.S., State) or State Parkway 20 5
State Boat Launching Site	

didn't arrive until 1651. Settlement began in 1789, mostly as a fishing town. Brewerton has had an up-and-down relationship with the canal. The original Erie went south of here, through downtown Syracuse. A side cut between the lake and the canal opened in 1835 developed Brewerton into a boat building center, but it was abandoned in 1863. The town benefitted again when the modern Barge Canal came through here in 1917. It is again a center for boating, but now for fishing and pleasure craft, with marinas, boat dealers, and repair yards not only clustered in Brewerton, but virtually ringing the entire lake. Brewerton is also the fortunate beneficiary of that key to twentieth century prosperity: an exit on the interstate--number 31 on I-81. The interstate connection makes Brewerton so convenient to Syracuse that summer evenings see boaters and fishermen fleeing the metropolis for a little recreation after work and before dinner. If your plans call for heading north on the Oswego Canal, access to Syracuse may be more convenient from Brewerton than cruising on to Liverpool or Syracuse.

The canal leaves the river at Light 159, 1.7 miles west of the Brewerton Terminal. You can motor northwest up the river channel as far as the dam in the little village of Caugdenoy. From Light 159 cruise another 1.7 miles to Lock 23, by far the busiest lock on the entire system. Through this little seven foot lock pass long distance transits from Lakes Erie and Ontario, all the main line traffic in this part of the system, fisherfolk and pleasure boats back-and-forth from the Syracuse basin at Onondaga Lake. From here on it's uphill all the way west; this is the last down lock on the way to Lake Erie. There's a Canal Park here with tie-ups, picnic tables and grills, rest rooms, pumpout. If you want to see a great big bunch of different kinds of boats in a little bit of time, this is the place to lay out your picnic spread.

The junction with the Oswego Canal at Three Rivers Point is eight miles west of Lock 23. Seven Locks (numbered from 1 to 8, but there is no Number 4) drop you 118 feet to the level of Lake Ontario in just 24 miles. If the Oswego Canal is your route, turn right at Three Rivers Point and turn to the next chapter.

74

Past Three Rivers Point, enter the Seneca River, at the level of Onondaga Lake and Syracuse. After holding a westerly course for so long, the change to a southerly heading is kind of nice...if you're sensitive to that kind of thing! To reach Onondaga Lake and access to Syracuse, head south at Klein Island to the lake outlet, under the Thruway, past the Park at the entrance, and into the lake. Klein is an artificial island, created during the Erie's latest re-incarnation. The Seneca River dips into a southerly bight just north of the lake; the straight northern channel was dug to cut off the loop, creating the "island." If you enter in Spring or Fall, Syracuse University racing shells might be speeding right by. Onondaga Lake has a long tradition hosting collegiate rowing events. In years past, railroad flat cars were equipped with bleacher seats so spectators could be chugged along tracks parallel to the race course for a commodore's eye view of the action. It wouldn't work now because scrabbly growth and trees have created a thin green border between railroad track and lake.

A Barge Canal Terminal lies close to downtown Syracuse via a half-mile channel from the southern end of the lake, but it's not the nicest neighborhood for a tie-up. Redevelopment plans for the area are in the talking stage. The port of choice for most visiting yachtsmen is the Onondaga Lake Marina in Liverpool, close enough to be convenient to the city. The park has recently been developed into a handsome setting. Onondaga Lake should be a jewel but its waters have been shamefully abused. The setting, with the city as a backdrop, is really very inviting. An eight mile recreational parkway for bikes, walkers and a tram, partly circles the lake. (Plans call for extending the trail completely around.) In late July there's a four day Onondaga Lake Waterfront Extravaganza with fireworks, specialty foods, games, water ski show. There are two "must" see destinations located in the Park: the Salt Museum and Ste. Marie among the Iroquois. Ste. Marie is a living history experience of French and Indian daily activity 300 years ago, exhibits changing with the seasons. The Salt Museum is about the central economic driving force behind Syracuse's modern industrial evolution.

75

THE NEW ERIE CANAL

Simon LeMoyne, a French Jesuit, is credited with discovering salt springs in 1654, shortly after the missionaries arrived. (I always wondered why the Indians who lived here for so many years had not "discovered" salt?) In any event, commercial development did not begin until 1788, slowly at first. Salt production rose steadily and eventually became an enormous business. During the mid-1800's the state received more than half its revenues from the salt tax alone. The business peaked in 1862, during the Civil War, and slowly declined after. Salt was important to the old Erie: as a valuable commodity to be transported, and as a preservative for all the beef, pork and fish packed in barrels and floated to market. The Salt Museum has audio-visual presentations, displays and models. One of the exhibits is a full-scale replica of a boiling block from 1856.

I have heard, and have no reason to believe otherwise, that Syracuse University students--the ungrateful whelps--call this city, the "truck stop."

It's easy to see why. Syracuse sits at a gigantic highway crossroads. There is a lot of trucking because of its location as a distribution center and its strong industrial presence. In spite of the fact that there are something like 600 manufacturing businesses here, Syracuse is more of an industrial survivor than an industrial juggernaut. And now-a-days, folks, that's as good as it gets. The city's vitality as a regional cultural and political center (over 1500 lawyers!) is apparent, but its real logistical value comes from sitting astride north-south Interstate 81 and east-west Interstate 90. In the heyday of canal transportation, Syracuse had the same transportation advantage--north to Oswego and Lake Ontario, south to the Finger Lakes, east to Albany and New York, west to infinity. Railroads quickly made this a large switching center. The same beneficent topology that favored canals, railroads and highways, was, of course, long utilized by the Indians: north-south tending valleys offered canoe routes to the south, river access to the Great Lakes, and a straight shot via Woods Creek down the Mohawk to the Hudson River.

Syracuse is a great place to live. It's one of those "mid-size" American cities. Big enough for a rich cultural life. Small enough so that big city problems are not so overwhelming as to have numbed citizens into helpless permanent stupor.

The old Erie Canal flowed through what is now downtown Syracuse. Filled in and paved, it is now appropriately called Erie Boulevard. Many of the same commercial buildings that lined the canal stand today. Most of these buildings still have two facades: prosaic work-a-day "front" (or was this the back?), often with characteristic cargo bays, facing the filled-in canal; on the other side facing the adjoining parallel street is a fancier "front" that looks like a first class business address of the late 1800's. And on Erie Boulevard East you'll also find the Erie Canal Museum. This should be a stop for anyone with even the most casual interest in the history of the canal and its impact on New York and the nation. The museum is housed in an old weighlock building, one of the structures originally used to weigh cargo and charge tolls. A loaded freighter would enter a "weighlock". Water would be drained from the short lock, and the entire boat weighed on a balance beam scale. Similar weighlocks were located in Rochester, Utica, Watervliet and Albany. Tolls were based on weight, commodity and distance. Captains complained, calling weighlocks "guessponds" and claiming that the dry weighing damaged watertight integrity of their boat. And yes, even cheating occured when goods were loaded and unloaded before one of the 17 toll collecting stations was reached. Collectors were overworked and underpaid. Nobody ever seemed happy with the arrangement. Over the years rates declined due to pressure from shippers and competition from railroads. In 1883 tolls were abandoned altogether.

You can board a full-size canal boat in the Museum, and view fascinating exhibitions of construction, commodities hauled, economic impact, migration patterns, and a range of changing audio-visual productions. If it has been a few years since you last visited the Museum, call in again. The entire presentation has been greatly improved and enhanced. Mostly, there is a great "feel" to this museum, probably because it is not a replica or reproduction but the real thing. You can sense the rumble and roar of long dead locks filling and emptying. The Erie Canal Museum also operates Canal Center, located in DeWitt at the end of the Erie Canal State Park. A small gift shop has a unique selection of books and tapes. At Erie Boulevard East and Montgomery St. (315) 471-0593. P. S. If you're running around downtown Syracuse, try to be there on Tuesday, at S. Salina and Washington Streets, on farmers' market day.

Perhaps it has occured to you that interest in the Erie Canal is almost a local industry. Well, you'll be convinced when you learn that there is one *more* Erie Canal Park. It's in Camillus, about five miles west of the lake. This 300 acre area has seven miles of usable canal and trails along the old towpath, period buildings, a lock-tender's Shanty Museum, nature walks, boat tours, and picnic areas.

The New York State Fair is held in Syracuse every year in early September at the State Fairgrounds, on the western shore of Onondaga Lake. It would be nice just to cruise on over there, tie-up and visit the Fair. But you can't. Like so many other attractive events and places that *should* be accessible from the water, the State Fair has made no provision for the boater. For a free brochure with this year's dates write to New York State Fair Grounds, Syracuse, NY 13209.

A Travel Guide about Syracuse/Onondaga County with all sorts of information about accommodations, tours, shopping, historic and natural sites, events, festivals, etc. is available from the Syracuse Convention & Visitors Bureau (315) 470-1800; events information: (800) 234-4797

Returning to the canal from Onondaga Lake, you can take the port tack around Klein Island to rejoin the Erie headed west. There are two marinas to starboard once back in the canal, J & S and River View. From this level it is all uphill to Lake Erie. Lock 24, 11 foot lift, at Baldwinsville is 6.4 miles from Onondaga Lake outlet. There's dockage above the lock on the north side of the river. This is a nice little village of about 6,000, pleasant enough for walking around. Cooper's Marina, (315) 635-7371, a full service facility with 10 transient slips, is conveniently close to restaurants, diners, fast food, motel and a laundromat.

The settlement was started in 1797 when Dr. Jonas C. Baldwin, traveling to Seneca County, stopped at the rapids with his family. They were on the way to settle property in Seneca

County. But the doctor saw an opportunity in the drop of the river here. The river had been chartered by the State to the Western Inland Lock and Navigation Company for development of a canal from the Mohawk River and Woods Creek, into the Finger Lakes. Dr. Baldwin acquired Western Inland's rights to the Seneca River. The company was never successful with their canal and eventually sold out to the State. By 1809 Dr. Baldwin, with a State charter, was able to build a dam and a lock on the river. With the water power, Baldwinsville began to develop as a mill town. Although the town was by-passed by the original canal, navigation on the Seneca River later made a connection with the Erie at Three Rivers Point. During the late 1800's the town included four mills, a pump manufacturer and a steam engine factory. By the time the modern Barge Canal was constructed, most industry had faded away.

At this level of 374 feet above sea level, you have a nice long run of over 34 miles from Lock 24 to the Junction with the Cayuga--Seneca Canal. Not a lock in sight. At least, not a modern lock. You have entered a peaceful, bucolic countryside, heading west passing the Howland Island State Wildlife Management Area, and dropping into a southwesterly direction before entering Cross Lake. The lake is about a mile wide and four miles long in a north-south direction. There's a "Big Island" as you enter the lake and another, "Little Island" in the middle just south of the east-west channel. Make the passage north of white buoy which is 500 feet north of "Little Island". Most of the lake, however, is navigable. Cross Lake marine is tucked into the very northwest corner of the lake; a restaurant is adjoining. It is 22.5 miles from the lake's exit to Lock 25.

Weedsport comes up about 10.5 miles after re-entering the canal. The Thruway has an exit here and Route 34 runs right through the middle of town. The original Erie also ran right through the middle of town, but now the canal is about a mile north. There are tie-ups at the Midway Marina, about a half mile east of Route 34, and at the Riverview Hotel and Marina. Accommodations at the Best Western and the Port 40 Motel. This village, like so many others, had its ups and downs tied in with the canal. About 1800 an inn had been located here.

79

The first completed section of the canal, 94 miles from Utica to Montezuma, created its own boomlet when it reached the village in 1820. Cayuga County has a hike and bike trail along the old towpath from Schasel Park in Port Byron to Centerport Aqueduct Park, a mile west of Weedsport on Route 31, where there's a re-built section of the old canal. There's also a museum-- the Old Brutus Historical Society, on North Seneca St., open Wednesday and Sunday from 1 - 4 pm.

Port Byron--about three miles south of the intersection with Route 38--is another community by-passed by the Barge Canal. The State has a boat launching site 11 miles west of the lake exit at Howland Island, northeast of the Howland Island Bridge. This area marks the eastern edge of Montezuma Marsh. Eagle Bay Marina is at this location. About .8 of a mile before the junction with the Cayuga--Seneca Canal are magnificent sections of aqueduct from the first rebuilding. This span, completed in 1856, was originally 900 feet long. When the canal was installed in the Seneca River, the central piece was demolished.

I realize that some call going into the Cayuga--Seneca a "side trip." But don't think of it that way. You could spend a happy Spring-Summer-Fall in those, the two biggest, Finger Lakes. When you are ready for the Finger Lakes, be prepared to spend some quality time. Then turn to Chapter VIII. But for now, here we are, lifting six feet at Mays Point Lock 25 and headed west on the main line, along the northeastern edge of the Montezuma National Wildlife Refuge. You can tie up above or below the lock.

Canal construction techniques were fairly well-developed by the time digging started on this section of the canal in 1820. However, the swamp presented its own set of difficulties. In those days the swamp was a much larger area of land. Its present greatly reduced size was caused by damning the outlet of Cayuga Lake during the modern rebuilding of the canal. The work had to be performed in the water, usually in up to a foot. Sickness struck widely. Practically every contractor's work crews became ill and schedules lagged. Nevertheless, by 1822 the canal was completed through the swamp. When drained, this black mucky soil makes outstanding agricultural land. Potatoes and celery grow particularly well. At one time clouds of waterfowl came through here but the loss of Cayuga's flood, farming and development reduced the habitat. In 1937 the Federal government set aside over 6,400 acres--a remnant of the swamp's original size--to form the wildlife refuge. Civilian Conservation Corps crews built levees and dikes to hold water in certain areas. It has proved to be a successful experiment. Even eagles have returned. Sizable flocks of migrating ducks now come through here in the fall. No hunting in the refuge, of course, but hunters have a good ol' time on the periphery of the reserve. Lock 26 is straight ahead, 8.3 miles west of the Cayuga--Seneca Junction, on a steady northwestern course. If you are not at the helm, grab the binoculars. This is fine birding territory. There can be a lot of genuine peacefulness on this leg of the trip. You are here because you want to be here. There is only one bridge between the locks, at County Line Road. A short walk to the east brings you to a ditch, all that's left of the original. Another few minutes east discloses a piece of the 1862 re-construction. It's an easy little walk; tie up by the bridge.

Lock 26, another six foot lift, and only 2.5 miles to the village of Clyde. You can make fast under the Glasgow Street bridge on the south pier. Several restaurants, laundromat, groceries, and antique stores are clustered close-by. As may be implied, the village was settled by Scotsmen. The major industry for over 100 years was a glass works; an old mill on Sodus Street now houses a museum enthusiastically operated by the Galen Historical Society. (315) 923-3971 In the next 31.5 miles, from Clyde to Lock 30 in Macedon, the Erie jogs north and south, and passes eight parks, a nature center, a wildlife area and one museum plus the historic sites of the Mormon Church in Palmyra. Several of the parks are county-run. They are here by the old canal largely for the local folks and visitors from anywhere. I take such a concentration as a sign of welcome for the water-borne traveler. Combined with the hike and bike trails, the parks are really an extended recreational right-of-way.

Lyons, and Lock 27, is almost 11 miles from Clyde. This is a 12.5 foot lift. This is the county seat of Wayne County and one of the first sights you'll see--from miles away--is the bright dome of the court house. Like so many other towns and villages in this part of the country, Lyons was settled in 1789, after the Revolution and westward movement of whites was permitted. You can tie-up on the north wall. The Wayne County Museum (315) 946-6191 is right by on Butternut Street. Groceries, restaurants and laundromat in the village; the closest marina is Miller's, a half mile west. The State maintains a dry-dock facility at the next Lock 28A, 2.3 miles west of the Lyons lock. There's a 19.5 foot lift here, followed in 4.5 miles by 12 feet at Lock 28B in Newark. The first round of plans during the modern re-building of this section called for only one lock with a lift of 31.5 feet. That height of lift--though not the highest on the canal-- and other constraints, convinced engineers to re-design with two locks. In the meantime a new lock numbering system had been assigned throughout the Barge Canal so that Lyons and Newark wound up with an A and a B.

The canal runs through a marsh section for over three miles--flanked by uncharacteristic hills-- coming into Newark, the largest city along the Erie between Syracuse and Rochester. A Canal Park--this one operated by the county--is located right at the lock; moorings here, electricity too. About two miles north of Newark is where Spiritualism started in the Fox home. The Fox family, after moving into the house, began to hear shoveling in the cellar, dragging sounds and knockings. The daughters are supposed to have begun communicating with the spirit on March 31, 1849. The spirit told the youngest girl that he had been a peddlar, murdered there four years earlier. Nightly disturbances and the press of the curious forced the family to move to Rochester where, the story goes, the encounters took on a diminished form. There is not much to see at the site now, the house having been removed by a spiritualist group to Lily Dale, on Lake Erie. There are shops and a Sheraton Inn nearby along North Main. (315) 331-9500. House's Motel is close-by too on Route 31W. (315) 331-0768. A couple of good restaurants in town including one at the Sheraton, plus the fast food burger stores and a pizza chain. It's very interesting--and a lot of fun--to visit the Hoffman Clock Museum in the Public Library. The two old Erie Canals run parallel here, the 1862 construction being the favored route now for the continuation of the hike and bike trail.

The hike and bike trail follows the river coming into the Widewaters, something of an aquatic recreation area, marked by white nun buoys. There's a little picnic area, with rest rooms and a sandy beach, where the Widewaters begin. Stay to the north; the south shore has a lot of cottages along it and small craft activity.

Before coming into Wayne County, you may have noticed the very unusual shape of Cayuga County, like of long pointy finger reaching north, getting skinnier by stages, and finally dipping into Lake Ontario. Years ago when they had the political clout Cayugans wanted very badly to reach that lake. It's kind of the same thing in reverse here in Ontario County at Port Gibson, with a half-mile of south bank tangentially touching the canal. The folk of Ontario County wanted the canal very much too and somehow (could it have been a needed legislative vote?) engineers magically moved the planned route into a graceful southerly bight to call at Port Gibson, Ontario County.

Lock 29--16 foot lift--and the uniquely historic village of Palmyra are about 11 miles west of Lock 28B. Swift's Landing (the original name of Palmyra) County Park is about two miles east of the village. The hike and bike trail continues to shadow the canal through this section, making it an ideal stretch for walkers or bikers to go ashore and loosen up. It's a brief walk into the village if you tie up at the Railroad Avenue bridge, or you can make fast at the lock. Aqueduct Park at the lock is built around the remnants of the original span carrying the canal over Ganargua Creek. The Church of Jesus Christ of Latter Day Saints was founded here by Joseph Smith in 1830. His home on Stafford Street, an 1820's farm, is open for free daily tours. Sacred Grove, where he had his first vision, is near-by. In 1935 Mormons erected the Angel Moroni Monument four miles south on Route 21. The Hill Cumorah Pageant, one of the country's largest outdoor religious presentations, is held here every August. If there's anyone on board interested in the arts and crafts of quilts and rugs, be sure to stop by the Alling Coverlet Museum on William

Street. (315) 597-6981. There are restaurants, stores and laundromat in the village, and the Canaltown B & B on Route 21. (315) 597-5553.

Continuing west to Macedon--canal and constant commpanion hike and bike trail--Lock 30, State Canal Park and hamlet are reached in 3.3 miles. The Canal Park is typical of the State-run parks--picnicking, parking, pump-outs. About a mile east of the lock, in a little north shore inlet, sits an old Erie lock, complete with wooden gates. If the pace of riverine activity seems to be picking up, it's because we are practically in the suburbs of Rochester, perhaps New York's most dynamic city.

Chapter VII

Oswego Canal: Three Rivers Point to Oswego and
Lake Ontario; Locks 1 to 8

A world of adventures await the end of only a short cruise north on the Oswego Canal to Lake Ontario.

Cross the lake to spend a summer in Canada.

Visit Toronto, a beautiful, authentically multi-cultural, cosmopolitan, welcoming city on the northwest coast of the lake.

Run up the Trent-Severn Canal to Georgian Bay and Lake Huron's north channel.

Or take the Rideau Canal from Kingston to Ottawa.

There is the magnificent possibility of summer in the Thousand Islands!

Set a westerly course and enter Lake Erie via the Welland Canal.

Enter the St. Lawrence Seaway and head for Montreal, an enticing destination at any time of the year.

Return to the Hudson River via the Chambly Canal, Richelieu River, Lake Champlain, and Champlain Canal.

The grand adventure starts by turning right at Three Rivers Point.

This 24 mile canal in the Oswego River drops 118 feet through seven locks, all of which are on power generation. It is fully and reassuringly documented with NOAA charts, included when you order the "New York State Barge Canal System" set. The fishing is great for walleye, bullheads, pan fish and bass as you begin the trip, gets even better, and becomes sensational for trout and salmon by the time you reach the mouth of the river on Lake Ontario. Make the trip in late September or early October when the spawning run is on and it could be one of the fishing highlights of your life. Different tackle, different baits and lures, completely different techniques. Come prepared; this can be a fishing holiday in itself. In addition to good fishing, there are parks, even golf, attractive communities, and a welcoming attitude toward boaters in general.

This is a distinct geologic area, sitting to the west of the Tug Hill Plateau, not yet at the gradually higher elevations uplifting to the Adirondacks, but in the path of winter snows storming off Lake Ontario. Glaciers scraped this area, creating "hogback" hills to mark terminal moraines. There is a nice ruggedness to the countryside that comes from having been once wild, getting civilized and farmed, and now reverting to scrub and secondary forest. The bird watching is outstanding. Several years ago I saw my first ever eagle in New York south of Fulton.

The "Oswego Route" was one of the first early proposals for a canal, favoring access to Lake Ontario. Indeed, this was one of the main original routes for Indian travel, fur trade and military cammpaigns and was considered as an alternative to the straight route across the breadth of the state. The Oneida River, coming from Oneida Lake, and the Seneca River, originating in the Finger Lakes, meet at Three Rivers Point to flow as the Oswego during the short drop northward to Lake Ontario. The pre-canal route was by batteux or canoe. Generally, plans for the original Canal did not consider rivers as feasible for adapting to use as a canal. The large drop in the last 12 miles of the Oswego convinced the Commissioners that they would have to build a "horse railway" around the falls. This difficult drop on the Oswego and the formidable construction of a water passage on the lower Mohawk River between Schenectady and the Hudson River to reach Albany comprised the most daunting engineering challenges for overcoming abrupt changes in elevation. Many eastern and southern New Yorkers, apprehensive about competitive potential of undeveloped land in the western counties, favored a canal from the east to Lake Ontario. Others were genuinelly concerned that water-borne produce, once on the waters of Lake Ontario, would find its way to Montreal via the St. Lawrence and the overall commercial benefits to the State--and the country in the case of international trade--would be lost. The difficulties of moving meaningful volumes of cargo via the St. Lawrence seem to have never been fully understood by either side of the debate. Montreal, too, was at a competitive

86

Oswego Canal

Lake Ontario

3

104

104

Mexico

11

104

Fort Ontario
State Historic Site

Wrights Landing
Park

104

81

8

7 6 Oswego

Parish

H. Lee White
Marine Museum

Oswego

5

104

104

Oswego

Battle Island
State Park

3

Canalview Marina

Canal

3

Fulton

3

264

49

Hannibal

Lake
Neatahwanta

Oswego Canal
(Abandoned)

Central
Square

Big Bay State Wildlife
Managment Area

Curtis Gale
State Wildlife
Managment Area

River

481

Phoenix

Henley
Park

Brewerton

23

49

Three Mile Bay State Wildlife
Managment Area

176

Three Rivers
State Wildlife
Managment Area

Greene
Pond

1

Three
Rivers Point

State Canal
Park

Onondaga
Shore Park

Oneida Lake

370

48

31

Seneca

370

24

48

31

Lions
Community Park

River

481

Clay Marsh State Wildlife
Managment Area

11

31

481

Liverpool

81

90

90

Onondaga Lake

90

LEGEND

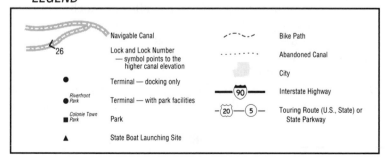

Navigable Canal	Bike Path
26 Lock and Lock Number — symbol points to the higher canal elevation	Abandoned Canal
Terminal — docking only	City
Riverfront Park Terminal — with park facilities	90 Interstate Highway
Colonie Town Park Park	20 5 Touring Route (U.S., State) or State Parkway
State Boat Launching Site	

THE NEW ERIE CANAL

disadvantage with eastern American ports by sailing ship times delivering wheat to Europe.

From Three Rivers Point to the Lock Street lift bridge is almost four miles. Tie up by the bridge for convenience items close by. Henley Park is located in Phoenix just before Lock 1, where a drop of 10.5 feet begins the descent to Lake Ontario. There is some room for anchorage in the basin north of Walter Island, 2.8 miles north of Lock 1.

The thriving city of Fulton comes up 10.8 miles north of Lock 1. Locks 2 and 3 are here with successive drops of 17.8 and 27 feet. Make fast at either lock but Lock 3 has a small overlook park and is closer to restaurants. The Canalview Marina is located on the eastern shore between the locks. One of the nice things about navigating in a canal is that you can take what comes. So don't go looking for Lock 4. There never was one on the modern Oswego Canal, just something included in the engineering plan but as construction neared the need for a "Lock 4" proved unnecessary.

Watch for Pathfinder Island about 1.3 miles north of Lock 3. According to local lore, this is where James Fennimore Cooper's hero Natty Bumpo fights the Iroquois in his famous novel "The Pathfinder". Stay in the channel; it quickly becomes shoal draft and marshy around the island.

About halfway between Locks 3 and 5 is Battle Island State Park, complete with a golf course! There's a hoist and ramp available at Vacation Harbor on the eastern shore just south of the Battle Island for which the park was named. On July 3, 1758 the French and Indians were beaten off here after attempting an ambush of a party under the command of Colonel John Bradstreet. From Lock 3 it's a run of 7.3 miles to Lock 5 where a 19 foot drop brings you even closer to Lake Ontario. Lock 6 is almost in the city of Oswego, followed quickly by 7 and 8. Lock 6 is a 20 foot drop; Lock 7 is 14.5 feet; Lock 8--by now you can see Lake Ontario--is 11.1 feet. This is the only siphon lock on the entire canal system and was designed like one in Germany on the Keil Canal. It is also the largest of this type in the world and the first of its kind to be constructed in the United States. The full-service Oswego Marina is located to

88

Coming into Lake Ontario from the Oswego Canal.

starboard just out of Lock 8 (315) 342-0436. Plan on spending some time in this interesting city.

The fascinating and educational Energy Center at Nine Mile Point, six miles west of Oswego, is operated by the New York Power Authority and Niagara Mohawk Power Company. Allow at least two hours to go through the self-guided tour. For information write to: The Energy Center, P. O. Box 81, Lycoming, N. Y. 13093 (315) 342-4117.

Fort Ontario is an historic site operated by New York State Parks and Recreation. The existing re-construction is of a star-shaped major fort that originally dated from 1759. The structure of the fort, the living quarters and surroundings are all highly interesting. The museum is one of the most engaging military collections you'll find. The Army post of Fort Ontario actually stayed in active service until recent times and the museum documents its many functions from wilderness frontier fort to World War II. It was even in use during the Civil War when the Union feared an attack from Canada while its attentions were involved elsewhere.

89

Old barracks at Fort Ontario.

Capture the character of this region's rich maritime history at the H. Lee White Marine Museum. You'll find ship models, historical exhibits, and artifacts covering a 300 year period. It is open from Memorial Day to Labor Day. (315) 343-4503

The historic Richardson-Bates House Museum is a meticulously preserved Victorian "Tuscan Villa." Part of the house is maintained as the original residents lived and the remainder is devoted to local history. It is also the headquarters of the Oswego County Historical Society. (315) 343-1342

Sport fishing on Lake Ontario is a sizable local industry. This is authentic trophy fish country...coho, chinook, steelhead salmon. Sign up with an experienced charter skipper and be fairly certain of not getting skunked. Of course, fishing is never "for sure", but the waters around here are the among the best you'll find in Northeastern North America. There is even a Fishing Hotline: (800) 248-LURE. For a travel guide and more information, write to: Promotion and Tourism, County Office Building, Oswego, N. Y. 13126. (315) 349-8322

Chapter VIII

Cayuga--Seneca Canal: From The Montezuma Wildlife Refuge to Cayuga Lake and Ithaca; to Seneca Lake and Watkins Glen; Locks 1 to 4

Few non-boaters know that you can board a vessel in say, Vermont or Long Island, and cruise into the two largest Finger Lakes. And actually, most boaters don't realize that this kind of extended cruising exists. A trip into the Cayuga--Seneca is often called a "side-trip." What a side-trip! It's a show in itself.

The entrance to the Cayuga--Seneca Canal is 1.5 miles east of Lock 25 on the New Erie or 1.3 miles west of the launch ramp and marina by the Route 31 bridge. Practically as soon as the Cayuga--Seneca is entered, you pass under the New York State Thruway.

This is grand, just great cruising country for the tourist/yachtsman. The Finger Lakes are a delightful, self-contained vacation in themselves. Some folks come back year-after-year to the campgrounds and motels; others manage to get a shore-line cottage and come back every year.

Without exaggeration, the water-borne vistas in much of this territory are stunning. As great as life on the water is, there are many other attractions here, so allow plenty of time and don't ever think of this as just a "side-trip." If you only want to make a short excursion into the Cayuga--Seneca Canal, go through the Montezuma Swamp and stay overnight at Seneca Falls. But don't tease yourself by entering either lake, because you'll just want to stay and then feel badly if you can't because you didn't put enough time into your plan. Besides, this is the kind of place to savor, deliberately falling into its slow, soft and naturally mellow rhythm. Although you are never far from civilization, there's a certain peaceful majesty in the Finger Lakes environment.

Once into the lakes, marinas abound. Think about

stepping the mast and raising a sail. The canal puts you into only two of the Finger Lakes but these are the largest two. Long, but hardly ever over two miles wide. There are city-type destinations at the southern ends--Watkins Glen and Ithaca but not really much along the shores. There are shore-side State Parks, fine fishing and some pretty good golfing along the way. About mid-way down the west side of Seneca Lake is Dresden where the early canal had a connector into Keuka Lake at Penn Yan. Keuka had been known as Crooked Lake and the connector was called the "Crooked Lake Canal." Keuka is a pretty lady, and I've never thought of her as "crooked", but more as a split lake with two northern arms. Remnants of the Crooked Lake Canal can be seen along Keuka's outlet; it's grand to day-dream about how nice it would be if that connector were still open.

The bicycle is a natural adjunct to boat or automobile travel through the Finger Lakes. The surrounding hills may seem daunting from water level but they don't climb forever, and once climbed--or started out on from auto--are very gently rolling roadways. Actually, the Finger Lakes are ideal bike touring country: spectacular scenery, good roads without heavy trucking, many state parks and campsites, easy access to provisions at many small villages and plenty of bicycle shops.

The Cayuga--Seneca Canal is not one but actually two short canals split into the Cayuga and Seneca branches. The cruise begins where the junction is in the Montezuma National Wildlife Refuge. The refuge has an extremely interesting Visitor Center where you can learn a lot about what the refuge actually is, how it came to be rescued from devastation (just barely) and a lot about the ecology of the resident and transient wildlife-- particularly birds. It's close enough to the canal, but with no formal boating access. However... If you want to visit the Visitor Center informally, here's how: Anchor just south of the busy bridge carrying US 20 and Route 5, near the launch ramp and Fishing Access Site. Walk a few yards to the highway, cross it, and there's the plainly marked road to the Visitor Center, which is about one-eighth of a mile north of the highway. It's only about one-eighth of a mile west of the canal too but don't try to bushwack your way cross-country. It's not allowed! The

Cayuga-Seneca Canal

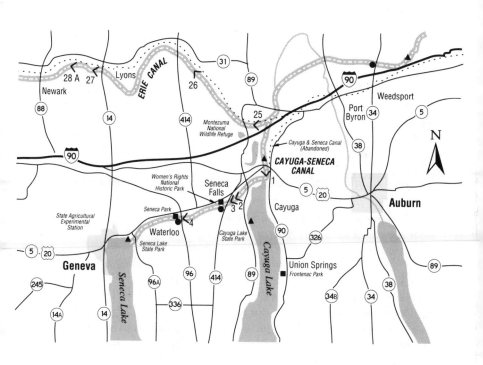

Lyons
28 A 27
Newark
88
14
ERIE CANAL
31
26
414
Montezuma National Wildlife Refuge
89
25
90
Weedsport
Port Byron 34
5
Cayuga & Seneca Canal (Abandoned)
90
CAYUGA-SENECA CANAL
38
Women's Rights National Historic Park
Seneca Falls
1
5 20
State Agricultural Experimental Station
Seneca Park
3 2
Cayuga
90
326
Auburn
4
Waterloo
Cayuga Lake State Park
Seneca Lake State Park
N
5 20
Geneva
245
Seneca Lake
96A
96
414
89
Cayuga Lake
Union Springs
Frontenac Park
38
89
14A
14
336
34B
34

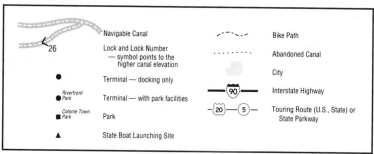

LEGEND

26	Navigable Canal	Bike Path	
26	Lock and Lock Number — symbol points to the higher canal elevation	Abandoned Canal	
●	Terminal — docking only	City	
● Riverfront Park	Terminal — with park facilities	90	Interstate Highway
■ Colonie Town Park	Park	20 5	Touring Route (U.S., State) or State Parkway
▲	State Boat Launching Site		

THE NEW ERIE CANAL

Visitor Center is not shown on NOAA Chart 14786. These are
my estimated distances; I didn't pace them off and I tend to be
optimistic.

Lock 1 is 4.5 miles on an almost-straight southerly run
from the entrance to the Cayuga--Seneca Canal. Its 8.9 foot lift
raises to the level of Cayuga Lake. Both Cayuga and Seneca
Lakes are included in the NOAA marine chart package as part
of the New York State Barge Canal System. The charts are
invaluable for navigation, show some marinas, but barely give
a clue to the many shoreline attractions. A couple of good highway
and tourist maps are necessary: The "Complete Map of New York
State," of course, as described in Chapter II and the very detailed
"Finger Lakes of New York State" from Marshall Penn-York Co.
at 538 Erie Blvd. West, Syracuse, NY 13204. (315) 422-2162.
This latter publication shows golf courses, marinas and boat
launches and is handy if you know where you are headed, not
as a source of ideas. However, it is truly indispensable for the
ambitious cyclist and backroads motorist.

The Finger Lakes make up one of the most desirable and
oft-traveled bike touring regions in the country. Many bike routes
are well-marked and until a few years ago the area was perhaps
the most well-documented bike touring in the U. S. A great free
publication--Finger Lakes Bicycle Touring Map--was available
free from the regional headquarters of New York Parks, Recreation
and Historic Preservation at Taughannock Falls, RD 3,
Trumansburg, NY, 14886. It comprehensively covered
recommended first and second choice bicycle routes, documented
bike paths and did it for not only the Finger Lakes per se but
adjoining greater Rochester and Syracuse. Grades were marked
along with practically every conceivable convenience for the
touring cyclist. A terrific resource! Archive copies exist but don't
even ask for a photocopy because the functional utility was in
the color-coded overlays onto existing roadways. The same
regional office does have some handy bicycle touring information
available. Write to them. They are thinking about trying to
get a corporate sponsor for their original 1980 map. It would
need some up-dating but, wow, what a nice start.

There is a little book called "25 Bicycle Tours in the Finger

94

Lakes," by Roth and Walters for $9.95 from Backcountry Publications, P. O. Box 175, Woodstock, Vt. 05091. . The tours are meticulously detailed and even if you're not biking it's worth it for the descriptions of attractions along the tours, historic sites, museums, and restaurants. The same publisher also does "25 Walks in the Finger Lakes Region" by William P. Ehling for $5.95.

Another fine publication that comes out every year for all tourists is the Finger Lakes Travel Guide, a rich resource of accommodations, marinas, shopping, campgrounds, golf courses, restaurants and more. It's free but there is a modest $2.00 handling charge if ordered by mail. From the Finger Lakes Association, 309 Lake Street, Penn Yan, NY 14527 . You can also write to:

> The Schuyler County Chamber of Commerce
> (Accommodations, Travel Guide, etc.)
> 1000 N. Franklin St.
> Watkins Glen, NY 14891
> (607) 535-4300

The junction with the Seneca Lake Branch is into the starboard channel soon after exiting the lock. From Lock 1 to Lock 2 in Seneca Falls, it's 4.3 miles. Locks 2 and 3 are one right after the other with lifts of 25.9 and 24.5 feet--an impressive gain in elevation.

Seneca Falls is famous as the birthplace of Women's Rights. Just to the south of Lock 3, a short walk up a little rise, is the Elizabeth Cady Stanton house, one of the principal leaders in the women's rights movement. Motor south through Van Cleef Lake, pass under two bridges and on the right is a small park and long wall for dockage. Maintained by the city--providing electricity and water--this nice little dock is virtually in the middle of town. Quiet enough, it makes a good overnight. The Women's Rights National Historical Park is literally directly across the street from the mooring wall, separated by the city's small canalside park and the main street. Don't expect a "park" at the Historical Park. This historic site commemorates the countrywide grass roots movement, with the leadership in Seneca Falls, when the cause of women's rights was first gasping for recognition. The organizational and structural struggle culminated with the first national convention for Women's Rights, also here in 1848. A Visitor's Center, maintained by the National Park Service, recreates the conditions of women's lives at the time the movement began and chonicles the historical development of the struggle. About a block down the street the National Women's Hall of Fame is located in what had been a bank building. Included here are exhibit biographies of the women selected for the Hall of Fame. Restaurants, coffee shops, pharmacies, laundromats and all the other conveniences are right at hand. There is an old hotel, maintained in the grand manner, located in the heart of the little city too. Motels and a larger choice of restaurants are outside of town to the west.

Lock 4 is last on this branch canal before reaching Seneca Lake. It's 4.8 miles from Locks 2 and 3 and is in the village of

Elizabeth Stanton Cady's house in Seneca Falls is a short walk from the locks.

Waterloo. Lift of 13 feet. A boat launch is just west of the lock. Memorial Day was first celebrated in Waterloo on May 5, 1866; and a museum devoted to the observance is located in the village. Two complete marinas are about 3.6 miles west on the north shore. From there it's about 1.5 miles to the northeast corner of the lake where the canal makes its entry, actually the river's exit. Seneca Lake State Park Marina is on the right and the Seneca Yacht Club is on the left. Seneca Lake State Park stretches along the northern shore; at the state marina you'll find water, electricity, pumpout, phone, showers, snack bar, etc. and it's close to a restaurant, laundry, groceries and bottled gas. The park borders Geneva, one of the bigger cities in the area. A popular tourist destination is the Rose Hill Mansion, notable for its Greek Revival architecture. Located at 543 S. Main Street, it houses the Geneva Historical Museum, replete with local history exhibits and Empire Style period furnishings.

You are now into great boating country There are 12 marinas scattered around the lake--sort of a gross indicator of just how great the boating is. This is a deep lake, 640 feet--in spots 200 feet below sea level on the bottom. Its cold water nurtures an outstanding fishery: lake, brown and rainbow trout, plus walleyes, northerns, bass and schools of perch. Sudden drop-offs make anchoring problematic. That's why so many boaters head for the recognized marinas with slips; have a plan. There are a lot of boats, but you'll never feel crowded because it is a big lake. The clear waters so rare in inland lakes make this an attractive destination for SCUBA divers who keep finding relics of the lake's early maritime activity. Watch for "DIVER DOWN" pennants.

The city of Geneva is tucked into the northwest corner of the lake, Watkins Glen and Montour Falls at the extreme southern end, Smith Park and marina in Hector on the eastern shore and Sampson State Park, also on the eastern shore. Watkins Glen is doubly famous--for its rich auto racing heritage, and for the awesome gorge exposing the ancient geological forces that shaped these valleys.

And then, there are the wineries! Over 25 wineries in

97

the Finger Lakes offer tours and tastings and 10 of them border the southern half of Seneca Lake. If Europe is said to be producing a lake of wine, and California a sea, then at least the Finger Lakes might be corking a large pond. Plan to visit a winery or two or three but please, please don't compare these winery tours to Napa-Sonoma. I have worked, traveled extensively, entertained and been entertained in the Finger Lakes for many years. And I have lived on the edge of Sonoma County. I love both places and want to be especially careful in delineating their differences.

True, this is the Number Two wine producing region in the country but it takes more than the mere width of a continent to explain the totally different ambiance between a Finger Lakes and a Napa-Sonoma winery. Not for one little second could I ever denigrate the quality of California's wines. Nor do I even want to compare them with the Finger Lakes'. California's wines are great! I just want to talk about the quality of the wine tour. In California it's a big deal; in New York it's no big deal. Touring wineries in Napa-Sonoma is the reason to be there; in New York, a winery tour is just one more nice thing to do on a much more varied outing. The wine sold from California's tasting rooms is a small fraction of production; in New York the wine sold direct from a winery often accounts for the entire production. While Finger Lakes restaurants compare well with others in upstate New York, California's wine country restaurants have their lineal ancestry in San Francisco! Although California has some nice little family wineries tucked away in the hills and side roads, for the most part the tour means charging up and down a couple of straight-as-a-die north-south busy-ways on flat valley floors. The pace can be frenetic. In New York you are present at an agricultural process--it could be cider. California presents a nicely-packaged, sanitized "visitor center" experience that is more marketing than agricultural! The bigger name wineries in Napa-Sonoma may devote their largest public space to the tasting and wine-selling room but the crush (honest, no pun intended) of people has encouraged them to set up boutiques and gift shops, blurring the focus on wine. In the Finger Lakes, the winery often is the boutique. Picnic grounds I'm all for, but T-shirt stalls? Gimme a break. Don't get me wrong, I love Napa-Sonoma wine but I've never understood what makes normal people go a little ga-ga over the "wine country." Probably because they have never seen New York's wine country. In the overall competition, the Finger Lakes get gold medals for laid-back ambiance and sheer physical beauty.

So how do you get at some of this gold medal material if you are coming in a boat?

Alice's Marina (607) 243-8461 and the Showboat Motel, near Himrod on the western shore, offer access to visit the Prejean Winery and the Four Chimney's Farm Winery. Prejean is about three plus miles from the water, on Route 14. It's a bit a huff and puff getting up the hill on a bike but not all that strenuous, and a hoot coming back down. Just ride carefully coming downhill, especially after the tasting rooms. (315) 536-7524 Four Chimney's is about a mile and a half--it's regularly walked from the marina--on Hall Road off Route 14. They also have an antique and gift shop.(607) 243-7502 The Showboat Motel (and Seneca

A rental boat from Mid-Lakes Navigation casts off from the public dock in Seneca Falls.

Landing Restaurant) is right on the water and provides tie-ups. Bicycles are available for guests. There's another good restaurant--the Gold Coast--about a half mile from the marina. This mid-lake area around Himrod is a proved fishing "hot spot". The Herman Weimer Vineyard, about 11 miles on Route 14 north of Watkins Glen, near Dundee, bottles wines and champagnes in the "European" tradition. (607) 243-7971 A little farther south (eight plus miles from the Glen) is Glenora Wine Cellars. (607) 243-5511 Giasi Winery, also on Route 14 and only three miles north of the Glen, specializes in a cherry dessert wine and red and white table wines. (607) 535-7785 Herman Weiner and Glenora can be reached calling in at Glenora, or coming up from the Glen; Giasi is easily reachable from the Glen.

Four wineries, listed here from north to south, are clustered in a three mile stretch around Hector on the eastern shore. Dunham's Marina (607) 546-2121 doesn't have slips for transients so the best bet is tying up at the Glen and taking a bike or cab. It's between Valois and Hector. The Hazlitt 1852 Vineyards Winery is on Route 414 between Hector and Valois. (607) 546-5812 Wickham Vineyards, Tichenor Road off of 414, produces premium wines, has tours too. (607) 546-8415 A new winery with a nice spirit is the Chateau LaFayette Reneau, also on 414. (607) 546-2062 Rolling Vineyards is only 7 miles from the Glen.(607) 546-9302

Farther north in Lodi on Route 414, about 15 miles from Watkins Glen, is Wagner Vineyards. The wines and views are both premium, produced in a unique octagonal pine and hemlock winery.(607) 582-6450 Access for boaters is from the Lodi Point State Marine Park. (607) 582-9904 It's less than three miles, uphill, so take your time because it is a scenic slog.

Sampson State Park on the eastern shore is on the location of a huge U. S. Navy Recruit Training base virtually built overnight during World War II. Many of the old roadways and buildings still stand. Sampson is what you might call a "full-service" park. There is just about everything here for the camper and the boater except a golf course. There are transient slips, water, electricity, campsites, pumpouts, showers, and a launch ramp.

CAYUGA--SENECA CANAL

At the extreme southern end of Seneca Lake, east of Watkins Glen, the Seneca Canal enters for a two mile plus run to Montour Falls where there is a 180 slip marina--no charge for tie-ups. Marinas in Watkins Glen and on the canal to Montour Falls can also accommodate transients. Watkins Glen, of course, is almost synonomous with U. S. auto racing. And there's the inspiring Glen Gorge and a nightly "Timespell" presentation. Chequaga Falls--almost as high as Niagara but with no where near the volume--is one of the main attractions in Montour Falls. The now abandoned Chemung Canal, on its way to Elmira and the southern tier, ran through Montour Falls' historic district.

The auto race track is about four miles west of the villages. Through the summer months, a full schedule of weekends is offered: NASCAR stock cars, Sports Car Club of America racing, endurance sedans, and special events. The track at the Glen has been extensively re-designed and is once-again a major auto racing attraction. Great care has been taken to make the events spectator-friendly and the area attractive for family camping.

For overall information on nearby accommodations, camping facilities, and race schedule, write the Schuyler County Chamber of Commerce, 1000 N. Franklin Sts., Watkins Glen, NY 14891. Ticket price information and availability inquiries should be made to Watkins Glen International, Box 500, Watkins Glen, NY 14891. (607) 974-7162)

One of the most spectacular attractions in the Northeast is the gorge in Watkins Glen State Park. Two miles of trails start off right on main street to wend in and around ravines, caverns and 19 waterfalls. Every night the gorge's geo-history unfolds in a unique hour-long presentation called Timespell. The 45 million year-old geological evolution of the gorge is told in a panoramic presentation against the backdrop of the gorge itself, using laser projections and striking special effects. There is a modest charge to attend and a reservation is needed. Call (607) 535-4960

To have entered Cayuga Lake rather than taking the

connector into Seneca, all that's required is taking the channel straight south after exiting Lock 1 on the Cayuga--Seneca Canal. Cayuga is a deep, beautiful lake too. The northern seven miles of the lake are shoal draft in many areas; use the charts and stay in the channel. The small town of Cayuga is just to the left of the channel after entering the main body of the lake. About 40 miles long and two miles wide, Cayuga's hypnotic attraction is the water itself and the symmetry of the surrounding hills. When driving north-south on the eastern ridges--if you're lucky enough to have that sixth sense for land forms--the unseen lake can be felt, out there to the west, over the next little rolling hill. And you know you are "high above Cayuga's waters."

Among Cayuga's blessings are lakeside state parks and marinas, world-class views, family wineries, and the cosmopolitanism of Ithaca, a major college town, also known as the "city of waterfalls."

Four of the state parks have marinas: Cayuga Lake, Long Point, Taughannock Falls and Allan H. Treman. Long Point is the only one without a pump-out. All have showers. Cayuga Lake State Park is on the far northwestern shore, about three miles east of Seneca Falls. Long Point, on the eastern shore four miles south of Aurora, is a great mid-lake stopover. Taughannock Falls, a pretty spot on the southwestern quadrant, offers access to the Americana Vineyards. The Allan H. Treman State Marine Park, tucked into the shore opposite downtown Ithaca, has a 400 boat capacity.

Commercial marinas in the northern reaches of Cayuga are Castelli's (315) 889-5532 and Troy's (also a camper park) (315) 889-5560, both about eight miles south of Lock 1.

One of the largest marinas (200 slips) on the lake is Hibiscus Harbor (315) 889-5008 by Union Springs on the eastern side.

Although Ithaca is the complete college town, it has a thoroughly maritime ambiance. The water is never too far and marinas and boats are a prominent part of the city scene. As one might expect in a sizable college town, there's a nice selection of very good, very reasonably-priced restaurants. You'll not find a better array of bookstores or newsstands in the Finger Lakes.

Take the tour of Cornell and walk through the gorge coming down from the main campus. I have visited and toured countless campuses. Well, 50 for sure. Maybe 100? The tour of Cornell was the best. Try to have your tour include the agricultural campus.

Another great stop about two miles south of Ithaca on Route 13 is Buttermilk Falls State Park for the views of the cascading waterfalls, pools and scenic settings. The entrance, coming by bike from the Ithaca marinas is still on the flat, but some busy roadways for a short distance demand caution...and a helmet.

There are seven wineries on Cayuga's western shore and one south of Ithaca. All are family owned. In most cases their wines can only be obtained at the winery, or at restaurants and liquor stores in the area. It has only been a few years since New York repealed an anachronistic holdover from old "blue" laws to allow retail sale from the winery. Now we can savor their wine-making skills while admiring their entrepreneurial success.

Three estate bottlers are close to Romulus: Lakeshore, Swedish Hill and Knapp.--all wineries The dock at Lakeshore Winery-Antique/Craft Shop (315) 549-8461 draws four to 4.5 feet but there's anchorage for deeper drafted vessels. The Swedish Hill Vineyard (315) 549-8326 is about two miles from the water and can be reached from the small private dock at the end of County Road 124. Knapp Vineyards (607) 869-9271 is on the water but has no direct access. You can anchor and come ashore at Dean's Cove, a half mile south of the winery, where the state has a boat launch.

Plane's Cayuga Vineyard (607) 869-5158 near Ovid is on the lake but the shore line property stayed with the former owners when the winery was recently sold. Other than putting in at Sheldrake, about six miles to the south, there is no ready way to reach the winery. In the same area, getting to Hosmer's, (607) 869-3393 also requires the boater to run down to Sheldrake. No phones or cabs at Sheldrake either! Lucas Vineyards in Interlaken (607) 532-4825) can also be reached from Sheldrake. The Americana Vineyards Winery (607) 387-6801, a little farther

103

south, has no direct access but The Taughannock Falls State Park is only about four miles south. Three miles of that is mostly uphill.

Six Mile Creek Vineyard (607) 273-6219 is not directly accessible by boat but is worth the trip--six miles from Ithaca on Route 79 East. They have a surprising number of wines, beautiful views, picnic grounds. The Allan Treman State Marine Park is the closest large marina. If you are not relishing a six mile uphill bike ride, it's about ten minutes by cab from the center of town, about 15 minutes from Treman.

Many special events take place at these wineries--special tastings, barbeques, brunches, fish frys, cheese samplers, and at least two "Wine Trail" weekends each summer (607) 869-9271. The "Wine Trail" is a loose association of the eight Cayuga Lake wineries. A brochure with their annual calendar, addresses, and special event dates can be requested from:

The Cayuga Wine Trail
P. O. Box 123
Fayette, NY 13065

Chapter IX

Gateway to the West: Erie Canal, Fairport to Buffalo and Lake Erie; Locks 32 to 35

All right, what happened to Lock 31? Here we were cruising along back in Chapter VI, having just left Lock 30, drawing closer to Rochester, safe in the confines of a real canal, and we lost Lock 31! It's one of those locks that never was. Designed into the twentieth century re-building of the canal, it was later found to be unnecessary, dropped from the plan, but the subsequent locks were never re-numbered.

Something else is missing from this leg of your trip across the state: there are no marine charts for the canal west of Lyons! The National Ocean Service of the National Oceanic and Atmospheric Administration has decided that you will be safe enough in the canal without a chart. After all, they must reason, it is awfully difficult to get lost. But that is missing the point. The charts are primarily for your safety, pointing out obstructions, channels, bridge and road crossings, possible anchorages and tie-ups, and communities along the way. Charts are the smartest way to make the passage because they make your life on board more predictable. I'm sure you'll make it safely to Lake Erie without charts; it just would be better with them.

This section is where the name <u>Erie</u> carries its greatest weight and significance. Some of the greatest political battles over the canal originated in this region. The arguments were always economic and somethimes patriotic, such as Lake Erie and New York vs. Lake Ontario and Canada. Many thought that by ending the canal in Lake Ontario, the natural gateway to the world would be down the St. Lawrence to Montreal. Lack of adequate engineering and geographic knowledge, as it always does, put all kinds of wild and crazy arguments into the debate. The advocates of a St. Lawrence route were not one whit worried about navigating down to almost sea level at Montreal from Lake Ontario, a mere 245 feet higher. On the other side of the debate,

Gateway to the West

Lake Ontario

Lake Erie

Golden Hill State Park
Lakeside Beach State Park
18
18
Barker
Lyndonville
Wilson
269
63
27
18   Wilson Tuscardora State Park
148
425
104
Four Mile State Park
Youngston
93
78
104
271   Medina Terminal   Bike Path
Joseph Davis State Park
Middleport   Canal   31
18
Lewiston
104
James Upson Park   Erie   Medina
Lockport   34   Nelson C Goehle Municipal Marina   31A
Earl W Brydges State Artpark   35
Devils Horn State Park   Power Reservoir   77   63
91
Reservoir State Park   Iriquois National Wildlife Refuge
Whirlpool State Park
425   Tonawanda State Wildlife Management Area   Oak Orchard State Wildlife Management
Niagara Falls   78   93   Oakfield
Buckhorn Island State Park   93
North Tonawanda   N   26
Niagara Reservation State Park   Packet Inn Sweeney Street Park   Gratwick Riverside Park   West Canal Marina   Akron   77   63
190   Longs Point Park
Big Six Mile Creek State Boat Basin   Isle View Park   Nia-Wanda Park   Ellicott Creek Park
GRAND ISLAND   290   Tonawanda   Williamsville   5
Beaver Island State Park   324   Kenmore   324   90   33
5   33   Corfu
BLACK ROCK US LOCK   33   33
Theodore Roosevelt Inaugural National Historic Site   Depew   Lancaster   Alden   20
BUFFALO   190   90   90   20   20
90

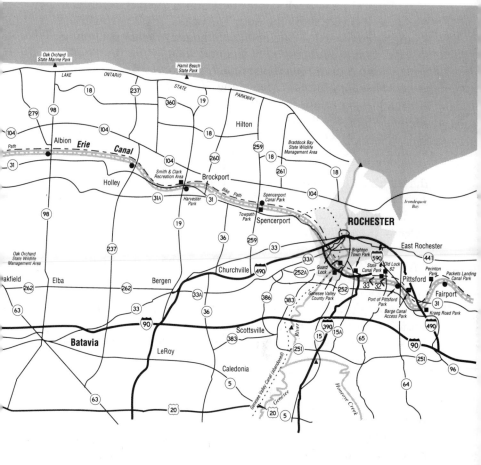

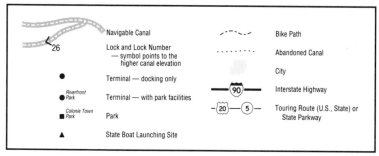

LEGEND

Navigable Canal	Bike Path
Lock and Lock Number — symbol points to the higher canal elevation	Abandoned Canal
Terminal — docking only	City
Terminal — with park facilities	Interstate Highway
Park	Touring Route (U.S., State) or State Parkway
State Boat Launching Site	

there was well-founded concern that not keeping the movement of goods within New York would give Canada distinct advantage. And even if Ontario was the route to the sea, there was still the daunting challenge of getting over Niagara to reach Lake Erie and the vast inland empire of the mid-west.

One of the proposals seriously put forward was to build the canal as a gigantic inclined plane. Not a series of little planes scaling modest ridges but one massive chute without a lock in sight. Forget about locks and run it downhill from Lake Erie to Hudson's River. The lake had plenty of water. Of course, it would have been tough getting the boats back up to the west.

Political finagling for location was vigorous throughout the length of the canal but was especially fierce in the west where gigantic tracts of land were owned by powerful economic interests. In the east and central regions of the state, many parcels had already been sold off and holdings were smaller.

Today there are only four locks in over 90 miles on this entire western section of the canal. But in the 76 miles between Fairport and Lockport you'll encounter 16 lift bridges. From Lock 30 to the Fairport Yacht Club it is about four miles, then another 4.7 miles to the Fairport Marina. This is not too early to start thinking about where you'll spend the night if its going to be anywhere near here. Despite its many attractions, Rochester is a thoroughly modern American city, e. g., dominated by the automobile. What this means to the canal cruiser is that no matter how serene your view from the water, you are sometimes only feet from a busy roadway. As the canal circumnavigates the southwestern quadrant of its loop around Rochester, it is hugged by Interstate 390, a busy, busy high-speed highway. A generous buffer of trees, shrubs and all manner of leafy things generally muffles the harsher roar but their is a residual hummmmm, hummmm. A strange juxtaposition, a sort of twilight zone. Get out of your car, walk a few feet, and you are literally a century in the past. That's great for the folks who come down here to run, walk, picnic, watch the boats, or ride a bike. They, however, go home to sleep while many of these roads stay busy well into the night... and water-borne quarters may not be as sound-proof as an airport motel. Also, there just aren't that many convenient overnight tie-ups or anchorages available in this rather large area. Actually, it's quieter at night in <u>downtown</u> Rochester than it is on the noisy expressway-bound periphery. Rapids, waterfalls and a dam, however, keep you from boating all the way downtown on the Genessee. Once you get as far down the river as you can go, there are plenty of tie-ups. No overnights but it's inexpensive and a bus line is close by.

Rochester has been called America's first boom town. From a small frontier settlement in the late 1700's it grew into a flour milling center with abundant water power and wheat from the Genessee valley.

Locks 32 and 33 are closest to the city and they provide overnight tie-up, pump-out, water, and a cosy nice picnic area. A cove just west of Lock 32 has additional anchorages. But...heavy traffic is not that far away. The best overnight amenities are

The Sam Patch, an excursion boat on the Genessee River, passing the University of Rochester campus.

THE NEW ERIE CANAL

in the pleasant suburbs of Fairport or Pittsford. Excellent restaurants are close-by and shopping for provisions and necessaries couldn't be more convenient.

The original site of Fairport sort of migrated from the hamlet of Perrinton to be closer to the original Erie. It was a nice stopover known as a "fair port." How fitting to revive a reputation--possibly 170 years old--because the locals wanted to be a "Fairport" to modern day canallers. Lucky you, the tie-up wall is practically in the middle of the village.

You can get a lot of useful mileage from your bicycles in this entire great leisurely northwesterly loop around Rochester and far to the west. In certain sections, bicycle and walking paths are on both sides of the waterway. Although it's not readily convenient by bicycle, there is a large shopping center in Bushnell's Basin. The commercial life of the area is mostly office parks close to Interstate 480.

Try to visit Richardson's Canal House Inn for great French regional and American country food. Built in 1818, it's listed on the National Register of Historic Places and is reputed to be the oldest surviving canal tavern. (716) 248-5000.

Going through Bushnell's Basin, I've been struck by the "European" view in the gracefully curving sections of the canal. You know you're in America by the design of the bridges, but the ambience is strictly France. It's also a strange sensation for the waterway to be running along above the roadway, where the canal is on the 80 foot Irondequoit embankment. In 1974 construction crews digging under the canal pierced its bottom, ripped a 100 foot breach, and drowned 40 houses. Miraculously, no one was killed. The entire episode is eerily like the worst imaginings of the canal commissioners back in the Fall of 1822 when the first embankment over the creek was constructed. They drained the just-completed superstructure every night and watched it closely during the day for fear a mighty leak would wipe out the farms below. Traversing the Irondequoit here, crossing the Genessee River just to the west, and scaling the Niagara escarpment were formidable engineering challenges to be overcome before reaching Lake Erie.

While wood, stone and earth elevated the canal above

110

the Irondequoit Creek, the Genessee was being crossed by cut stone and bolted bars of iron. Nine arches with 50 foot spans formed one of the longest aqueducts on the canal, a total distance of 802 feet.

A first attempt to cross the Genessee with an aqueduct was wiped out by a surging ice-filled river in the winter of 1821. The long arched span then erected looked sturdy and it was an impressive sight. But it had serious engineering and design faults. The sandstone foundation blocks soon began to disintegrate; the overhead structure leaked; a 17 foot width over the river restricted traffic to one-way; and a 90 degree turn was required of boats approaching from the west to enter the aqueduct. Its replacement was one of the priorities in the first re-building of the canal and in 1838 work began on a 45 foot wide by 848 foot long span of marble quarried from near Syracuse that is still standing.

Even before the western bank of the Genessee was reached, water from the river opened the canal eastward to the Seneca River, making 180 miles of navigation possible all the way to Little Falls. Wheat that had been selling in Rochester for $0.25 a bushel was now getting $1.00! This entire area would soon become famous for the quality and quantity of its farm products. By 1840 Monroe County was producing a million bushels of wheat annually; similar production was coming from the surrounding area plus impressive harvests of oats, barley and corn. This vast granary, about 40 miles deep, stretched from Cayuaga County to Lake Erie. By 1835, 21 mills made Rochester the country's flour miller, and, until 1844 the city's flour was the most valuable commodity shipped on the old Erie. Abundant water power and the canal's cheap and efficient transportation also quickly developed the wood-working industry. Timber floated down the Genessee to become finished lumber, barrel staves and furniture. As other flour milling centers later gained ascendency--mostly Buffalo with grain from the Great Lakes--Rochester's industrial base was in place as the foundation for even more dynamic growth. Clothing and shoe manufacturing were given impetus by the Civil War. In modern days, Rochester is synonymous with world leadership in photography, optics, and reprographics. Eastman

THE NEW ERIE CANAL

Kodak is still headquartered here but Xerox, after growing to its present stature, moved to Connecticut several years ago.

The New Erie Canal is at the same level as the Genessee River and the two meet at a crossing more like a railroad crossover than a watery confluence. It is even called a "junction".

Caution: <u>the river can generate a strong current.</u> The crossover is at the southwest corner of lovely Genessee Valley Park and cruising from there down to the central city is just as pleasant a side cruise as you can find on the system, but don't try bucking a heavy current. There are guard gates in the canal on both sides of the river, normally kept raised but operated if the river level has a marked change, making boaters "lock through."

Just north of Genessee Valley Park and to the east of the river is the campus of the University of Rochester. There are some small boat tie-ups and a canoe put-in right on the campus--a stone's throw south of the chapel. You can walk around this classy acreage, and visit the Memorial Art Gallery at 500 University Avenue (716) 437-7720. There's a visitor kiosk across from the chapel.

Although the end of river navigation is well-marked with white buoys, approach the downtown tie-up with caution. Stay to the west and maintain control.

Even though much of the commercial activity is now in the prosperous suburban office parks, Rochester does *have* a downtown and there is a lot to see. To appreciate the activity, try to visit on an ordinary weekly workday. It is really kind of dead on the weekend. There's the Rochester Museum and Science Center at 657 East Avenue (716) 271-4320. A few blocks east at 900 East Street is the unique George Eastman house, which attracts visitors from around the world to its International Museum of Photography (716) 271-3361. At Manhattan Square in the heart of downtown you'll find exhaustive Americana collections at the Strong Museum. Long a favorite with locals, this remarkable museum has gone largely unappreciated by tourists (716) 263-2700. For a complete packet of tourist information write to: Greater Rochester Visitors Association, 126 Andrews Street, Rochester, N. Y. 14604-1102 (716) 546-3070.

Pittsford, another of Rochester's attractive suburbs,is

a delight to visit. There's a park with tie-ups and electricity hard by the Main Street bridge. You can walk everywhere--to good restaurants, stores, craft and antique shops. Period architecture in the village makes the visit even nicer.

Leaving Rochester, the canal continues in the same broad northwesterly sweep, slowly returning to the bucolic ambiance of Upstate New York. West of Rochester the canal has been blasted through rock, interesting to look at, but cutting off views of the city's skyline. About 6.5 miles west of the "junction" with the Genessee River--where the canal turns westerly--a small cove on the north bank marks the original Erie's route into old time Rochester. Captain Jeff's Marina--a full-service facility close-enough to supplies--is about a mile west of the cove, on Elmgrove Road, a busy, very accessible north-south roadway, in the town of Elmgrove.

You are now on the longest continuous level in the system with no locks for 65 miles. This is pure canal territory...a man-made water passage that has long been a seamless part of the countryside. Now we have all these inland "ports" coming up, and a constant succession of bridges. The canal through this section was chosen for this more northerly route, as opposed to a southerly path through Batavia. As one would expect, the final routing was vigorously fought over. Buffalo interests favored the south because that would have assured termination in Buffalo rather than Black Rock. Available water supply dictated the final decision. The southern route closely paralleled the state highway, would have served several already-developed communities, been cheaper and shorter... but required rising 75 feet above Lake Erie. Even though the selected route uses water from Tonawanda, Skejaquada and Buffalo Creeks, the canal was designed with a drop of an inch a mile from the Niagara River to Lockport, making sure Lake Erie's abundant though fluctuating waters could be tapped when needed.

It's only about 3.5 miles from the cove marking the old Erie route to Rochester until Spencerport, another attractive suburb, comes into view. You can tie-up by the Canal Park or by the liftbridge; both have electricity. There's also a small boat tie-up at a next-door tavern. Walk to stores and a restaurant along Union Street; another restaurant is in the shopping plaza farther south.

Adam's Basin, about four miles west, has something that many canal enthusiasts think we should have more of: a canal inn functioning for its original purpose. Starting in the mid-seventies (1970's, that is), as bike trails were planned, canoe races sponsored, canal parks started and waterfront restoration organizations organized, the thinking went something like this: Wouldn't it be grand to have these old canal hotel-taverns once again serving real meals and accomodations to the long-distance bicyclists that would soon be using the trails. It didn't work out that way. The cyclists were interested in day trips with the kids and most of the old canalside hostelries hadn't been maintained anywhere near par for attracting the business of us modern-day travelers, spoiled rotten by squeeky-clean, characterless, chain motels.

Adam's Basin is the exception. Here there is the Canalside Inn, a bed and breakfast complete with tie-ups and nicely housed in an 1827 tavern. Tie-ups are also available approaching the lift bridge. It's a small town, but there is a deli on Washington Street and, of course, the Canalside Inn for meals. On the way to Brockport, the Adams Basin Marina is west of town at the intersection with Gallup Road. Brockport, a little over four miles from Spencerport, is a college town, part of the SUNY system with a State University College. College towns *are* different. They usually have more restaurants, at least one good bookstore, a movie theatre, and lots of fresh beer. That's what you'll find here too. Tie-ups are on the south wall, by the park. There's also a museum, above the library, with very interesting exhibits on local history. Brockport's greatest claim to historical fame is Cyrus McCormick's invention of the mechanical harvester. Although the machine has been given credit for the phenomenal development of American agriculture in the Midwest and Great plains, Western New York itself was the breadbasket of the country back then.

From Main Street in Brockport to Main Street in Albion it is just a shade over 16 miles. The canal meanders gently west, passing the hamlet of Hulberton. There are tie-ups here and further west by the Hindsburg Road and the Fnacher-Brockville Road. About five miles along the way lies the pleasant village of Holley, named after one of the hard working proponents of the original Erie. Myron Holley, confederate of DeWitt Clinton, land holder and Legislator, vigorously promoted the interests of the region and became one of the first Canal Commissioners. A short walk from moorings by the lift bridge takes you to shopping in the quaint town square.

Albion--the Orleans county seat--also has places for shopping, along with a fairly wide selection of places to eat, motels and a B & B.

Albion is home to one of America's famous inventors: George Pullman, who invented the railroad sleeping car, is reputed to have conceived his idea by observing the night arrangements on canal packet boats. Just looking at the restored packet boat in the Canal Museum in Syracuse, it is immediately apparent that--although Pullman cars incorporated some ingenious engineering-- the famous railroad sleeping car is a lineal descendant of the canal packet boat. Pallet-type bunks fold out of the wall, one-on-top of the other, with a drawn curtain for privacy. Pullman was a cabinet maker here from 1848 to 1855, then moved to Chicago and by 1858 was building the first rail sleeping cars. He became wealthly by actually operating and managing the cars; the railroads hauled the cars around the country for a fee. Pullman cars had a reputation for consistent high quality. In the mid-1950's the New York Central, ostensibly to save money, tried operating their own sleeping cars. Poorly maintained and manned by indifferent attendants, the cars soon became smelly and unkempt. In defense of the New York Central it should be pointed out that even though the company was notoriously mis-managed, they were successful in their goal of driving away what few passengers were left.

Until the 1920's, quarrying of Medina sandstone was a major local industry. Canal freighters floated this highly desirable building material away to major cities for buildings, bridges and architectural achievements throughout the country and even overseas.

Eagle Harbor comes up in three miles; tie-ups next to the lift bridge. Another three miles to the village of Knowlesville, with tie-up by the lift bridge and groceries on Main Street. Just about 1.3 miles west of Eagle Harbor, there's a cove for anchoring. At Medina the canal becomes an embankment and takes a southerly loop to cross over Oak Orchard Creek and Culvert Road. Although it is common for canals to pass over roads on the waterways of France, this is the only such crossover on the New York system. Dock at the Medina Marina where there is a park, water, electricity. Restaurants, groceries, motels and a B & B are all close-by. As the canal continues westward the favorable elevation on the embankment offers marvelous views and provides a good feel for the land form on this sweeping lake plateau. There are some highway locations that offer similar views along this way, but none quite as serene as the panorama from the deck of a canal cruiser. Halfway from Medina to Middleport, is the hamlet of Shelby Basin, and then Middleport with more restaurants, a motel and campground.

The Gasport Lions Memorial Park is 12 miles west of the Medina Marina. You can dock right there; water and electricity. The Widewaters Marina is by the Canal Park at the intersection of Market Street.

Gasport was named by a small group of students from the new academy in Troy that was to become Rensellaer Polytechnic Institute. During the summer of 1826 they embarked with an instructor on what had to be one of the greatest academic field trips of all time. Their dormitory was a chartered packet boat, equipped as a laboratory, and loaded with provisions for a round trip on the brand new canal. The small party of adventurous student scientists and engineers set off to study the magnificent project and all of its workings. In a spot about five miles west of Middleport they learned of a strange flammable substance that bubbled to the surface. It was, of course, a type of hydrogen gas generated by decaying vegetation. The young scientists proposed calling the unnamed hamlet "Gasport" and the name stuck. Six more miles through beautiful farmland to the aptly named city of Lockport.

While contractors wrestled with the daunting section from Schenectady to Waterford in the East, mounting the Niagara

The old locks at Lockport are side-by-side with the two modern ones and used for overflow.

escarpment here was the last great engineering challenge on the original Erie. There's dockage both above and below the locks. Coming from the west, about a mile before the locks, the Widewaters Marina and Canal Park has transient tie-ups and restaurant--a good overnight choice. Tour boats that shuttle back and forth between the locks are also based here. Tie-ups on the north wall below the locks by the small park are possible but perhaps not as secure a neighborhood for leaving an unattended vessel. At times quite a bit of floating and half submerged debris can come this way. You can also tie up above the locks just past West Genesee Street. The park is the site of what was an extensive water-powered industry using the head developed for the locks. An ingenious tunnel through the rock delivered power to the north side where it was used and also transferred by equally ingenious overhead belts to the other side of the canal. You'll enter two gargantuan locks here, one right after the other. Each lock has a lift of over 24 feet; when you come out of the upper Lock 35 you appear to be entering a tunnel but it's actually the Main Street Bridge overhead. It is not a very long bridge--all it does is cross the canal--but at 452 feet it is wide! Local festivals are often held here; it's great--in the heart of downtown.

The western side of the bridge is a ring-side seat platform from which to watch the locking operations. You'll probably notice right away that Lock 35 has two upper gates; there is not another lock on the system like this. This unique design is a very serious precaution to protect the lock from being rammed by an eastbound vessel while the level is down. There are guard gates west of here but their operation is not instantaneous. Without being facetious, although Lake Erie is known as a "shallow" lake, it does have a lot of water. The thought of that lake rushing into a down lock is the stuff of nightmares. Hence two gates. No short cuts here; both gates are always operated. You may not notice the operation if you are locking through to the west but you will coming east because the western-most gate opens first. The original Erie had 10 locks here, a stupendous engineering achievement. The locking arrangement consisted of five locks side-by-side to permit simultaneous up and down lockings. The flight of five locks on the north side now being used as overflow is from the first rebuilding in 1862. This is an outstanding opportunity to study the meticulous stone work done in that reconstruction. At the bottom of the flight is a small museum in the unused power station. There are some very interesting visual exhibits and photographs of the modern construction of these two locks in 1919.

Lockport has an outstanding array of restaurants in all categories--fine, fast and family--from which to choose. In the fast department, there is even one called Submarina. Shopping is also plentiful with stores downtown and in shopping centers to the south on Transit Road. There's a hotel in town and several motels along South Transit Road. A complex of historical buildings is located at 215 Niagara Street, operated by the Niagara County Historical Society (716) 434-7433. An aptly titled brochure "Historical Museums of Niagara County, New York" is available by writing to The Niagara County Federation of Historical Societies, 3531 Ewings Road, Lockport, N. Y. 14094

The immediate area has a prosperous and dynamic industrial base of manufacturing, food processing, chemicals and steel.

For the next six-and-a-half miles the canal travels the immense rock cut that was the last obstacle of the original Erie.

Work started here in 1822 but proved too massive for the small contractors. Seven miles had to be cut through the ridge, two of the miles through solid rock. Consequently, the State became the contractor! This was probably the first time in the United States that a state took on the responsibility of primary contractor. The Commissioners hired over 1000 workers and engaged contractors to act as overseers. Blasting through the rock was an extremely tough and dangerous job. Laborers loaded the shattered rock into baskets that cranes literally lifted right over their heads. The cut was 27 feet wide, from 13 to 30 feet deep with a towpath "chiseled" into the side. Two years before the work had started, Lockport consisted of two cabins; by the time this section was finished the site had developed into a thriving village and was well on its way to becoming a real city. Tree trunks placed against Lockport's houses protected them from flying rock as the cut was blasted through the Niagara escarpment. Progress is recorded to have been frustratingly slow but the cut was completed in June 1825.

It is almost 21 miles from the last of Erie's locks to North Tonawanda and the Niagara River. Along the way is the hamlet of Pendleton, where the Hide-A-Way Yacht Harbor Basin, (716) 625-9666, has water and electricity. The West Canal Marina is in Martinsville off of Tonawanda Creek Road. The Creek was used as part of the original Erie, but then the canal moved to Buffalo during the rebuilding and back here in 1912. Still on the Erie in North Tonawanda there's High Skipper Marine (716) 694-4311 and Wardell Boat Yard (716) 692-9428. Mast stepping is available at Wardell's and a short run North on the Niagara at Smith Boys (716) 695-3472. After chartless navigating through the western section of the Erie Canal, you can now go back to the comfortable reassurances of marine charts. This section is 14822, part of the Great Lakes.

Tonawanda is a fine place to stop with convenient shopping, good restaurants and abundant overnight accommodations. The Historical Society of the Tonawandas is in an old brick railroad station at 113 Main Street has a fascinating display of early canal artifacts. The Tonawandas were once a huge lumber port, the source of oak sailing masts and a big supplier of barrel staves. The Herschell Carrousell Factory Museum on Thompson Street is another good stop. Head for Buffalo upon entering the Niagara River and be prepared for a strong current. The channel escapes from the river's rapids and enters the Black Rock Canal, with a five foot lift, southbound through Greater Buffalo. Beaver Island State Park (716) 773-3271 is enroute with good facilities-- transient slips, pumpouts, showers, etc. There are commercial marinas too: Anchor, (716) 773-7063; Placid Harbor, (716) 693-6226; Harbor Place, (716) 876-5944; Rich Marine, (716) 873-4060; and finally, Erie Basin Marina, (716) 842-4141, in a large municipal park. As close as you'll get to the business district, Erie Basin offers a range of facilities for the transient boater: two restaurants, showers, ice, mini-mart, marine store, fuel, ice, pump-out and a launch ramp.

This is the Niagara Frontier, a tourist expression but

more descriptive than "Greater Buffalo." Geographically, it's a big area. When the original canal was being planned it seems--given the limitations of the the barges of the day--that Buffalo would have been the logical engineering choice for the western terminal rather than Black Rock. But even back then politicians were able to overrule engineers. To settle the Buffalo--Black Rock argument, all kinds of compromises were attempted, some of them very innovative. Before the canal construction crews showed up in 1823, this was a small frontier settlement. The canal brought enormous prosperity to the area, greater than the wildest imaginings of investors and local boosters.

Despite the tired jokes about Buffalo, the area has much to offer: museums, parks, good restauants, zoos, art centers, aquariums, and a genuinelly rich cultural life. And of course, there's the big event--Niagara Falls. The people who live here, love it. Jobs, of course, have always been the main attraction of Buffalo. The canal itself was the first big impetus to Buffalo's prosperity. Coupled with its strategic location and the economic acceleration imparted by development accompanying the canal, Buffalo went on to become one of the country's greatest transportation centers, a grain milling behemoth, a major steelmaking site, and a manufacturing center of encyclopedic proportions.

Buffalo has a unique maritime museum. It's the Naval and Servicemen's Park situated on six acres beside the Buffalo River. The historical development of the U. S. Navy from the Revolution is portrayed by a series of 41 models. The outdoor displays are the real thing: Army tanks, Air Force and Navy jets, and three decommissioned ships--the destroyer USS The Sullivans, submarine USS Croaker, and cruiser USS Little Rock. There is a modest charge; it is operated by Buffalo and Erie County and is reputed to be the only inland naval park in the country (716) 847-1773.

Write Niagara Frontier Information Office, 107 Delaware Avenue, Buffalo, N. Y. 14202. (800) 235-6979 or (800) 458-8969 from New York.

Chapter X

Champlain Canal: Waterford, Saratoga, Glens Falls, Fort Edward, Whitehall to Lake Champlain; Locks 1 to 12

Adventure travel steeped in history. That's a fair description of the route North. Although the canal is only 60 miles from the Federal Dam at Troy to Whitehall and the entrance to Lake Champlain, this can be the first leg of a 270 mile transit to Sorel, Quebec and the St. Lawrence River.

Proceeding north of the Federal Dam (Lock Number 1) simply head straight north in the main river channel. (The Erie takes a port turn at Peebles Island.) The citified shoreline of Troy quickly turns rural and you are now on one of the most strategic thoroughfares of our early colonial and revolutionary history.

About half of the run to Whitehall--to Fort Edward--is in the river; the next 30 miles is dug canal. The locks are numbered from one to 12 but don't look for number 10. Eleven locks will take you to Lake Champlain. Number 10 is one of those planned locks that proved to be unnecessary.

Lock C-1 is 5.4 miles from the Troy dam. It's a little confusing. Lock 1 on the Hudson is a Federal lock and not part of the state system. When you travel the Erie west, lock E-2 is your first lift in Waterford. The Erie's planners deferred to the Feds and named their first lock Number 2. When you head north on the Champlain Canal, the first lock is Number 1, making it the second Number 1 in a row--but New York State Number 1, actually C-1 the way the locks are numbered on the system. Too many years have gone by to go back and tidy up the inconsistencies of locks with the same numbers and missing locks that have never been renumbered. We may think it's kind of sloppy but in another 100 years it will just be quaint.

Soon after entering this stretch of canal, a shore-side visitor will notice strangely ominous NO FISHING signs. "Fish from these waters," warn the signs, "have high levels of contaminants and should not be consumed". The contaminants are PCB's, known carcinogens, dumped into these otherwise clean waters in the Fort Edward--Hudson Falls area by General Electric a generation ago. That was, of course, before we knew how really bad that stuff is. Our beautiful river is still deadly poisonous because it's a hellish problem to clean up. The corporate executives, their scientific colleagues, and our elected and appointed politicians haven't been able to agree how to effectively clean it up (there have been lots of plans) or even how to pay for it other than to throw a few token dollars at the mess. In the meantime, don't eat the fish. Otherwise this is a beautiful trip.

Lock C-1 is a lift of 14 feet; the run to Lock C-2 is 3.8 miles; after the 18.5 feet lift you are at the Mechanicville level. This is a hospitable stop for boaters. You can tie up at the Municipal Marina without fee; water and electricity are free. It's an easy walk to restaurants, good shopping, groceries (there's a supermarket) and other provisions. A monument in the town honors Colonel E. E. Ellsworth, the first Union officer killed in the Civil War when he attempted to remove a flag from a hotel in Alexandria, Va.

Lock 3 is only a little over a half mile out of town and Lock 4 is about two-and-a-half miles. With a lift of 19.5 feet, Lock 3 is the highest on the Champlain.

Lock 4 has a pleasant canal park. A nature trail/walking path passes through the woods and along the Hoosic River which empties into the Hudson just south of the park area. It's an easy walk from the lock over to the village of Stillwater. Immediately after exiting the lock cut, there's a small marina on the west bank, smack in the middle of the village, that may have a free slip for an occasional transient. Launch ramp here too.

All the really important things are in the village: pizza place, convenience store and restaurant.

Stillwater's location on this main north-south travel route gave it great historic importance. In 1709 Fort Ingoldsby was built here. 1756 saw the erection of Fort Winslow followed by the construction of Montressor's Blockhouse and Storehouse

Champlain Canal

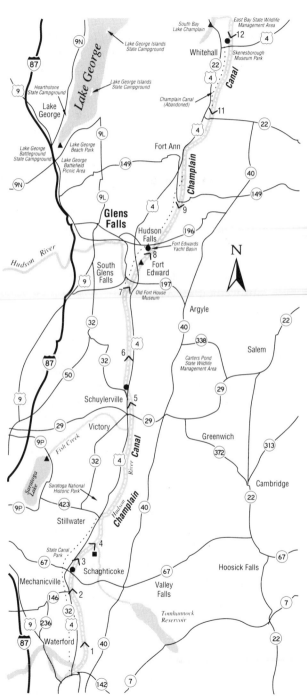

LEGEND

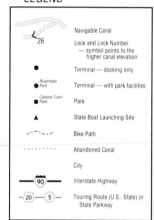

	Navigable Canal
26	Lock and Lock Number — symbol points to the higher canal elevation
●	Terminal — docking only
● *Riverfront Park*	Terminal — with park facilities
■ *Colonie Town Park*	Park
▲	State Boat Launching Site
----	Bike Path
······	Abandoned Canal
	City
90	Interstate Highway
20 5	Touring Route (U.S.. State) or State Parkway

South Bay
Lake Champlain

East Bay State Wildlife
Management Area

Whitehall

Skenesborough
Museum Park

Lake George Islands
State Campground

Lake George Islands
State Campground

Champlain Canal
(Abandoned)

Hearthstone
State Campground

Lake
George

Lake George
Battleground
State Campground

Lake George
Beach Park

Lake George
Battlefield
Picnic Area

Fort Ann

Glens
Falls

Hudson
Falls

Fort Edwards
Yacht Basin

South
Glens
Falls

Fort
Edward

Old Fort House
Museum

Argyle

Salem

Carters Pond
State Wildlife
Management Area

Schuylerville

Victory

Greenwich

Cambridge

Fish Creek

Saratoga
Lake

Saratoga National
Historic Park

Stillwater

State Canal
Park

Schaghticoke

Hoosick Falls

Mechanicville

Valley
Falls

Tonhannock
Reservoir

Waterford

N

Barracks in 1758. During the revolution General Phillip Schuyler located his headquarters and supply depot here. Schuyler's headquarters were in the Dirk Swart house, still standing and occupied as a day-to-day residence, a few paces from the small marina on the main road through town. Benedict Arnold, on his relief march to Fort Stanwix where the British were being held off, left from the Swart house. A short distance north on Route 4 a Revolutionary era tavern still stands in the hamlet of Bemis Heights, identifiable on the marine chart.

Revolutionary War history revolves around the British plan to split the colonies by driving down from Canada to New York, separating the fractious, unequivocally anti-Royalty Yankees of New England from the--it seemed to the British--less-fractious Continentals in the mid-Atlantic states who had a greater percentage of Loyalists. The battle at Saratoga is said to be the turning point of the war. At one time or another--they came and went--the Continentals had 13,000 troops and the British had 6,000. The skirmishes and attacks preceding the full battle were full of drama.

Political skirmishes on the Continental side were equally dramatic. Schuyler was relieved of command by Washington just before the British arrived and Benedict Arnold, unquestionably our greatest military field leader of the time, was relieved of his command by Gates, who had replaced Schuyler. Arnold was a hard man to keep down and even though he didn't have a command he saw an opportunity during the battle and led a successful charge. The military victory at Saratoga changed the entire course of the war--convincing the French and other European powers that we really had something going for us.

The main entrance to the Saratoga Battlefield National Park from U. S. Route 4 is about 5.5 miles on the river from Stillwater. Access to the Park is strictly for motorists but with a little ingenuity it's possible for the boater to get ashore and visit this magnificent national monument. An anchorage can be made off the east bank around the R "100" buoy on marine chart 14786 (C-3); a short gravel road leads to Route 4; the entrance road is directly across.

If you take a bicycle ashore, you're all set. The walk to

126

Looking east from the Saratoga Battlefield, over the Hudson River and toward Vermont. Anchorage possible near here.

the Visitor Center is easy enough but it takes a lot of getting around to really see the many battle sites. Easy enough on the bike, but a goodly hike. It's a 10.5 mile bicycle loop on the roadways through the battlefield, but only 4.2 miles on the Wilkerson Trail--a great recent innovation that takes advantage of short cuts for the walker. The Visitor Center is highly interesting in its own right with battlefield diaromas, Continental uniforms, weapons, military artifacts, brochures and literature. A 20 minute movie narrated by Burgess Meredith is shown at regular intervals. Wooded, shady picnic sites are located at the Visitor Center and at Stop 10 of the tour, about 8 road miles from the Center. This is really a great biking trip with fine scenery and only a few modest hills. On any nice day you'll see families picnicking and biking just for the fun of the area, and stopping to absorb some of the rich history. Detailed plaques at each Stop on the tour recount the action at that particular locale.

Other than attempting the improvisational anchorage across from the eastern entrance, there's a "Fisherman's Rest" Marina (with launch ramp) about 2 miles north. You can always tie-up along the wall below the gate at Lock 4, at the marina in Stillwater, or the public marina at Mechanicville. An admirable facility is the Schuyler Yacht Basin in Schuylerville, another two miles beyond the Fisheman's Rest. It's a reasonable cab ride from any of these places to the Battlefield. If you are driving, Route 32 provides a highway entrance on the west.

Schuylerville was the original Saratoga. Just south of the village is General Philip Schuyler's magnificant country house, unfortunately not now open to the public, but worth a visit. British General Burgoyne destroyed the original by burning it before he surrendered. This was rebuilt almost immediately under the supervision of Mrs. Schuyler. With great determination and resourcefulness--in the midst of a war--she obtained (perhaps "requisitioned" is a better word) the master building skills needed to complete such an impressive residence. Later, daughter Elizabeth married Alexander Hamilton here and George (he slept here) Washington came to visit.

The Schuyler Yacht Basin offers plenty of dockage for transients, although the fees are not cheap. There is a

Old lock next to the modern Lock C-5. General Stark held a position here to prevent British retreat to the north.

convenience store and restaurants of a sort within a short walk. The British surrendered on a parade ground here, grounding their arms but not being held prisoner. For all the brutality of life back then, things were certainly gentlemanly on the battlefield.

It's eight miles south to the Saratoga Battle Monument and 10 miles west to forever attractive Saratoga Springs. Here you'll find some outstanding restaurants and a delightful array of enticing shops. Bring money. But it's fun just to walk along Broadway, window shop and eat ice cream.

The New York City Opera comes to the Saratoga Performing Arts Center in mid-June; the New York City Ballet arrives in July; the Philadelphia Orchestra shows up in August; the Saratoga Chamber Music Festival is the first two weeks in August and the Newport Jazz Festival is late June or early July. And then there are special concerts for rock, pop and jazz fans. (518) 584-3330

The Fort Edward Yacht Basin makes a great overnight. Close to stores and restaurants and ususally busy.

THE NEW ERIE CANAL

Come in August when the horses are running at the flat track--an authentic piece of Americana in its own right. Want something special? Come for the early morning workouts. Breakfast available.

Saratoga abounds with hostelries but it would be awfully chancy--downright foolhardy-- to show up in August without a reservation.

Back in the Hudson River, it's about a mile to Lock C-5, lift of 19 feet, from Schuylerville. This section of the river is designed for canoeing. Close your eyes, concentrate real hard, and you can almost hear the quiet rhythmic paddling of Indians, French explorers and missionaries, and early Colonists, headed north and south on this busy passageway. The American General Stark took a position here to prevent the British from escaping to the north. There is a small park here and a few steps to the west of the modern-day lock is a fine example of a mid-1800's lock. The Batten Kill, a legendary trout stream that is fighting for its life from being loved to death by people pressure, empties into the Hudson after a clasically scenic flow down from Vermont. It's dammed entering the river and can't be reached from the channel.

About a half-mile north of Lock C-5 and opposite the upper dam is a seasonal produce stand on the west side of U. S. 4.

Lock 6, 16.5 foot lift, is the beginning of a 2.5 mile land cut. Tranquil enough, but--in case you haven't guessed by now--I prefer rivers, especially when they are so perfect for small boats as the Hudson is here. Seem from the roadways above, the land forms are beautiful here but you can't really get a sense of the quiet grandeur from the canal.

From Lock C-6 its a run of six miles to C-7 at Fort Edward, two in the land cut and four back in the river. You are now at the head of navigation on the Hudson. From here north to Lake Champlain the canal is all land cut. In the 1790's this was the same route marked out for the unsuccessful Northern Inland Lock and Navigation Company

In the days of canoe and batteaux travel, this was the beginning of the "Great Carrying Place" to Lake George. Look at this location on a map, taking into account the change in

Be patient making passage into Lake Champlain north of Whitehall. Once there, the views are spectacular.

elevation and the distance, and forever admire the strength and ability to withstand hardship of those earlier travelers who carried their heavy loads over this portage.

Looked at geologically, Lake George appears to be an extension of Lake Champlain itself--long, narrow, deep, north-south tending. That these were important bodies of water may be inferred from their namesakes: the British king and the most famous of the French explorers.

From Fort Edward, the Hudson moves into a sweeping, meandering southwestly climb past Hudson Falls and Glens Falls before turning north at Corinth to head almost straight north to its birthplace at tiny Lake Tear of the Clouds, in the heart of the Adirondack High Peaks. It was an amazing realization when VerPlanck Colvin, New York's first Surveyor General, learned that this small pond in a couloir just below Mt. Marcy, New York's highest mountain, was the origin of the Hudson River. Until Colvin's discovery, it had been believed and the maps showed

131

that Mt. Marcy drained north into the St. Lawrence. Colvin was extraordinarily excited by his discovery. How fitting: that New York's highest mountain should give birth to the Hudson River, virtually synonymous with the "empire" in Empire State.

The Yacht Basin at Fort Edward, in the channel to the left at Lock C-7 (10 foot lift), is sponsored by the local Chamber of Commerce, and what a nice job they do. A small park adjoins the long tie-up wall, right in the middle of town, and is a short walk to anything you need. No charge for the facilities. This is a popular spot in the boating season; there'll be vessels of every description, all over the place, and it's not really a large basin. During the summer months, the Old Fort House is open to visitors. Built in 1772-73 from timber salvaged out of a military hospital, it contains exhibits, dioramas, antiques of the colonial period. (518-747-9600)

Getting into Glens Falls or Hudson Falls is a bit of an ambitious uphill bike trip or a taxi ride for the yachting party. Glens Falls has an especially notable art museum that's worth the trip no matter where you start. It's The Hyde Collection of American and European art and antiques. Closed Mondays. (518) 792-1761 Also, try to visit the Queensbury Hotel, one of the grand old style that still functions superbly. A bike path from Glens Falls to Lake George takes you direct to beaches, picnic areas, historic sites and all the amenities of a popular vacation destination. From Fort Edward to Glens Falls, bike travel is along (some pretty busy) roadways.

From Fort Edward to Whitehall and Lake Champlain, it's all land-cut. Lock C-8, a lift of 11 feet, is 2.2 miles from Lock C-7. You are now at the height of land for the trip to Lake Champlain--it's all down-hill from this level. Lock C-9 drops 16 feet 5.8 miles from C-8. You'll barely notice Lock 10 because it was never built. Lock C-11 comes up a little over 9 miles from C-9; it's a 12 foot drop. The passage from Lock C-9 to C-11 takes you past Fort Ann. Just south of Lock C-ll is the Great Meadows Correctional Facility, the State prison at Comstock, a chilling sight. You really can't see the walls from the water but a short walk west of the bridge carrying Route 22 over the canal offers a horribly depressing vista. Quick, back to the boat.

132

Let me tell a fishing story.

A little over four and a half miles north of Lock C-11, the Mettawee River comes in from the east after flowing down through classically beautiful sub-mountainous and rural countryside. This is an exciting trout fishing stream and I can't pass it without this little anecdote. Several years ago I was having a pretty good day with ultra-light tackle. The fishing was so good that I didn't realize how tired I had become in the swift current until I stepped into a hole. My chest waders filled with water even though I had a belt up high. The stream has some deep holes. Scary, scary stuff. Quite a way downstream, my wife and a couple of the kids were picnicking with friends. First, they saw my hat go floating by. Then came my little canvas snack and soda bag. They thought that was kind of funny. Then I swept by in the fast current, completely out of control, half drowned but most of all worried about the new rod and reel I had lost. They thought I was funny too. And I never really tried to convince them that that little episode on the Mettawee was really a life-threatening experience.

The Champlain Canal ends at Lock C-12 right in the

Fort Ticonderoga is not to be missed. It's the kind of place you can go back to year-after-year.

middle of Whitehall. There is a long tie-up wall just above (south) of the lock on the west side of the canal. This lock is flooded from one side only; strong currents make it impossible for a small craft to hold fast to the west wall. It is mandatory that all south bound pleasure craft lock through on the east wall or raft against a boat on that side.

All the conveniences are here: restaurants, convenience and grocery stores, pharmacy, laundromats, and a nice, fixed-up little town. Masts can be stepped at the Lock 12 Marina, a few hundred feet after exiting the lock; food and lodging here too. (518) 499-2049)

The Skenesborough Museum is also here, within a few steps of the tie-up wall, bordered by a pleasant picnic ground maintained by the town. Whitehall is known as the birthplace of the U. S. Navy but after viewing the impressive honors paid to our early sailors at Annapolis and other sites, I wonder if the Navy knows that it was conceived at Whitehall. Here, the homage to our great Naval service is sincere, authentic, low-key and strictly local. In 1776 shipbuilding craftsmen from New England constructed our first warships here--either 12 or 15 vessels, depending on whose history you read. Under the command of Benedict Arnold, they successfully delayed the British from executing their plan of dividing the colonies that year. By the next year, the Colonials had gained considerable strength and organization and were able to defeat the British at Saratoga. The lake battle of Valcour Island is admirably depicted in a diaroma in the Museum. History of the Champlain Canal is also covered.

An outside shed covers the recovered hull of the original U. S. S. Ticonderoga, built at Vergennes, Vt. for battle during the War of 1812. This warsloop was MacDonough's flagship in the 1814 Battle of Plattsburgh. Its recovery in 1958 was a masterwork of marine archaeology. Open weekdays during summer but only on weekends after Labor Day. (518) 499-1155

The town of Skenesborough is named for Major Philip Skene, the original white settler, who lost his 37,000 acres when he remained loyal to the Crown during the Revolution.

Entering Lake Champlain--aside from the Great Lakes,

134

this is the largest U. S. lake-- is at first more like a river cruise along swampy shores. Stay in the channel. Gradually, a spectacular destination reveals itself. From different geological antecedents, Adirondacks look down from the west and the Greens from Vermont. Scenic and secure anchorages abound, but can fill up on summer weekends. At last count there were about 35 marinas. Launch ramps are located on both sides. Much of the surrounding land is wilderness but cottagers also occupy considerable stretches, so be careful and considerate. Among the close-by villages, there are many charmers. Plus, there are all the amenities of the attractive mid-sized city of Burlington. You can explore wilderness islands and the allure of fine dining all in the same afternoon. The lake even has its own well-documented monster--Champ. Over the years there have been several sightings and some blurry photos. Don't worry, Champ is friendly to boaters; just keep a camera handy.

Marine charts are essential for cruising this large lake and are not included in the New York State Barge Canal System collection. (The Canal ends at Whitehall.) You must order NOAA Charts numbered 14781 to 14784. Transit to the St. Lawrence needs Richelieu River Charts 1350 and 1351 from the Canadian Hydrographic Office. Navigate this lake intelligently. It is not only large, its topology is also complicated. Bays, inlets, and divided headlands are all part of its charm but also demand seamanlike respect. Watch the weather, and always have a back-up plan.

This entire area is equally spectacular for motoring or bicycling. Campgrounds, historic sites, accommodations and restaurants abound. Drivers can even get a little on-water experience with their automobile by boarding one of the cross-lake ferries.

As bicycle touring has come into its own in this country during the last 15 - 20 years, every year sees more cyclists circling Champlain. Vermont, of course, has long been great bicycle touring country and a little of that mystique has spilled down to the lake. But bike touring on the Vermont side of the lake is different than much of the rest of the State. Bicycling the Vermont shore is

Fort Ticonderoga's staff uniforms lend authenticity.

mostly flat, open terrain, past farms running down to the lake. New York's bike routes--like much of "inland" Vermont--are through hilly woodlands.

Be sure to include at least one lake ferry crossing in a bike tour of Champlain. You don't have to be a hard-core 100-mile-a-day biker. A fun trip is to make the ferry crossing, bicycle around for a few hours, have a picnic, and return on a later ferry. Three ferries operate in the northern end of the lake: Burlington to Port Kent takes an hour; 20 minutes between Charlotte and Essex; and 12 minutes from Grande Isle to Plattsburgh. Lake Champlain Ferries: (802-864-9804) At the southern end of the lake, where thirteen ferries operated in days of old, the Fort Ticonderoga Ferry survives to make a six minute crossing between Ticonderoga (Route 74) and Larrabee's Point in Shoreham. Entering from the south, and circumnavigating clockwise, you can call in at Westport, Essex, Willsboro, Port Kent, Plattsburgh (a sizable city--second largest on the lake) or Rouses Point all on the New York side. Major historical attractions are at Crown Point and Fort Ticonderoga, both fascinating places.

There's no practical dockage at Fort Ticonderoga but a growing number of boaters come to call each year. The anchorage is good, just dinghy ashore. The French had constructed their Carillon "stronghold" here in 1755, strategically placed above the outlet of Lake George into Lake Champlain. When the British under Jeffrey Amherst captured the site a year later, they renamed it Fort Ticonderoga. Early in the Revolution, Ethan Allen and the Green Mountain Boys first came to fame here when they surprised the British defenders with a night raid. Captured cannons were hauled overland to Boston (that's a story in itself) where George Washington used them to help drive the British out. In July 1777 the British under Burgoyne recaptured the fort. American attacks later that year were repulsed, but the British ultimately abandoned the site.

This magnificent national treasure has been preserved and restored because of the efforts and foresight of a private individual, William Ferris Pell, who acquired the fort in the last century. His descendants carried on his work of restoration for many years; today the Fort Ticonderoga Association continues a grand tradition.

One of the plaques at the fort gives an idea of its historical importance by listing names of the famous who passed through here:

George Washington	Ethan Allen
Benjamin Franklin	Seth Warner
Benedict Arnold	Major Robert Rogers
Horatio Gates	The Marquis de Montcalm
Anthony Wayne	The Duc de Levis
Arthur St. Clair	Sir Jeffrey Amherst
Henry Knox	Sir Guy Carleton
Philip Schuyler	Major John Andre
Richard Montgomery	Sir John Burgoyne

Thaddeus Kosciusko

"And a host of others..." as the memorial goes on to state.

Crown Point is readily accessible from the lake, there's a large, beautifully-situated marine campground, right on the lake and directly across the road the from historic sites. Crown Point doesn't have the museum or large intact structures of Fort Ti, but, because of the way the site is being restored, it's an absolutely fascinating look into early military engineering, presented in a professional manner that doesn't gloss over the technical details of early fortifications and the conduct of war.

Coming down the Vermont side, there's North and South Hero, St. Albans Bay, Mallets Bay, Burlington, Shelburne and Vergennes.

Burlington is an attractive city, a great place to live and fun to visit, hospitable to sailors and easy to get into and out of with some fine restaurants close by the waterfront.

If you plan to visit the Shelburne Museum, allow plenty of time--at least a day. This not a "pop-into, pop-out of" kind of museum. Notable collections are displayed in 37 historic and exhibition buildings over 45 acres. Guided tours are offered. (802) 985-3346

Vergennes makes a nice stop with a waterfall spilling practically into the public docks. A full-drafted boat will have to anchor out.

The Lake Champlain Maritime Museum at Basin Harbor has a fascinating array of nautical exhibits specifically pertaining to this historic body of water. Included are boats, a working forge, boat building exhibits. Tie-up at the Basin Harbor Club, North Harbor, or anchor out. Basin Harbor is an elegant family-owned private resort. It's open to the public for dinner--this is really something special. A tad formal. Reservations: (802) 425-3211

Self-guided tours of Crown Point explain the engineering of early military fortifications.

Chapter XI

Hudson River: Albany to New York City

Right from the start, especially if you are entering the Hudson from the north, it helps to understand that south from the Federal Dam at Troy it's technically a tidal estuary. From Poughkeepsie south the Hudson is brackish but fresh water inflows help to maintain a river current of about a half mile-per-hour. The tidal currents are more significant and should be understood for prudent and skillful boat handling. Docking and other maneuvers take on a new level of complexity when the effects of tide are superimposed on current and wind. And, as in other of the world's places subject to tides, you'll undoubtedly encounter the large ships that tides bring with them.

Understanding the stage of a tide and how it affects your boat is the difference between being a skilled river pilot and Sunday boater just hoping to get by. As for those ocean-going behemoths coming and going from the Port of Albany, just follow Fitz's First Fundamental of Fright-Free Flotation: GIVE WAY TO TONNAGE!

The Hudson River is not a part of the Erie Canal, old or new, but obviously without it there would have been no Erie and thus historically speaking the Hudson belongs in the same milieu as the canal. But the Hudson is a unique marine environment and more demanding of seamanship skills than the canal. Our purpose here is to describe access from the river to some of the Hudson's principal attractions and to offer a few caveats for boaters more familiar with the confines of inland river, lake and dug canal.

Marine charts of the Hudson are in nautical miles, while those of the canal are in statute miles. You'll need NOAA Charts Nos. 12343, 12347, 12348. Most marine dealers in the area also carry a composite chart on waterproof paper produced by International Sailing Supply.

To adequately write about navigation and marine facilites

on the river would require another book larger than this. There are two: Allan W. MacKinnon's "Hudson River Boating Guide," is an intimately detailed on-the-water guide to the river and its caprices with notes on marinas and comments on restaurants; "Boating on the Hudson THE GUIDE" is an exhaustive compendium of the river's marine facilities. There's also an authentically good guidebook--complete with history and restaurant advice-- called The Hudson River Valley, by Tim Mulligan; it's written for the motorist and has been updated since its first printing in 1981..

Headed south and once past the bridges of Troy, masts and standing rigging can be stepped. The channel widens after Kingston but there are opportunities for sailing. Mast work is done at Troy's Town Dock,(518-272-5341) under and just north of the Green Island lift bridge.

The Castleton Boat Club, (518) 732-7077 has do-it-yourself mast stepping, usually no transient slips, but moorings are most often available. Other possibilities for mast stepping/hauling are Finke Marine at Coeyman's,(518) 756-6111 and Riverview Marine at Catskill, (518-943-5311)   One caution: all the way from Albany to Spuyten Duyvil watch out for high-speed trains when you walk a few yards inland on the eastern shore. Amtrak passenger trains tear through here at well over 100 mph but only a few of the grade crossings are gated. Please be careful; these trains are on you in an instant with almost no advance noise to announce themselves.

Amtrak's Empire Service between Albany/Schenectady and New York City is a delightful way to see the Hudson River Valley. Get a seat on the right hand side going south.

Amtrak is not a commuter railroad but the service between Albany and New York City is swift enough to attract a crowd of regulars. It's often tough getting a seat, much less a good seat, on the early morning weekday trains!

At Hudson, 17 plus nautical miles south of Castleton and our first stop, a loyal band of early risers makes the two hour trip into New York City every day. Calling in at Hudson will give you an idea why some folks spend over four hours a day commuting for the opportunity to live in this unique little

Hudson River

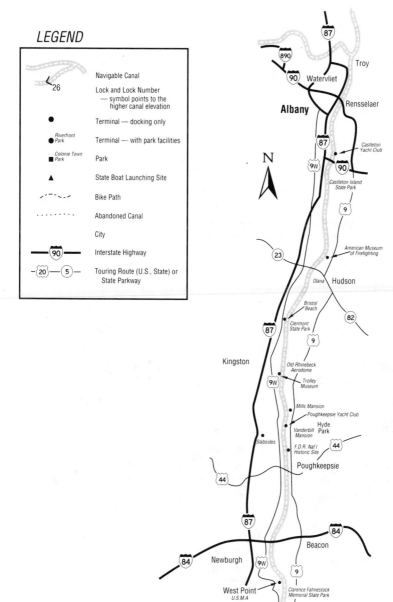

LEGEND

~~	Navigable Canal
26	Lock and Lock Number — symbol points to the higher canal elevation
●	Terminal — docking only
● Riverfront Park	Terminal — with park facilities
■ Colonie Town Park	Park
▲	State Boat Launching Site
- - - -	Bike Path
. . . . . .	Abandoned Canal
	City
═90═	Interstate Highway
—20——5—	Touring Route (U.S., State) or State Parkway

Troy

890

90 Watervliet

Albany

Rensselaer

87

Castleton Yacht Club

N

9W

90

Castleton Island State Park

9

23

American Museum of Firefighting

Olana Hudson

Bristol Beach

82

87 Clermont State Park

9

Kingston

Old Rhinebeck Aerodome

9W Trolley Museum

Mills Mansion

Poughkeepsie Yacht Club

Vanderbilt Mansion Hyde Park

Slabsides

F.D.R. Nat'l Historic Site 44

44

Poughkeepsie

87

84

Beacon

84 Newburgh 9W 9

West Point U.S.M.A.

Clarence Fahnestock Memorial State Park

day commuting for the opportunity to live in this unique little city.

Hudson earned its first niche in history by becoming a whaling port. That part of its background is included in the brochures put out by the the Chamber of Commerce. It's more recent notoriety as a bustling center of prostitution and gambling, however, is still unacknowledged in the tourist literature. Today, Hudson makes a great port of call for its magnificent surviving collection of early colonial homes, world-class antique shopping, and the American Museum of Firefighting.

The whale business started in 1783 when whaling families from Nantucket and other New England ports, fearing their home ports too exposed to still-hostile Brits, relocated to the secure confines of this friendly inland river.

The origins of the prostitution business are not so well documented but it flourished until 1950 when a reforming State

Hudson's early colonial homes makes this a great place for walking.

government swept into town, rounded 'em up, held trials, and sent some of the offenders--including several former local officials--off to prison.

Transients can dock at the Hudson Power Boat Association, close to the center of the city. A ramp is also located close-by at the Hudson Boat Launching Site. When the whalers came to Hudson, North and South Bays were true bays; construction of the railroad causeways cut off the bays from river scouring and allowed them to silt up.

Hudson as a community has survived some gritty times--including two horrendous fires--but the amazing thing is the survival of so many late 18th and early 19th century buildings in such a concentrated area. You can most appreciate Hudson by first obtaining a buff-colored pamplet "Historic Hudson--Colonial Restoration and Old Upper Hudson Walking Tours" available from the Columbia County Chamber of Commerce, 729 Columbia Street, Hudson, NY 12534. (518) 828-4417. This little booklet is an architectural house-by-house guide to the city's many

Hudson's own newspaper.

145

notable early homes and buildings, divided into two walking tours: a one-and-a-half-hour and a half-hour. Also ask the Chamber for "Hudson's Waterfront - A History", an unsigned, unacknowledged, un-annotated, stapled and very inexpensively produced, but highly interesting account. I hope it's still available.

The Robert Jenkins House and Museum on Warren Street, listed on the National Register of Historic Places, is a treasure chest of artifacts, art and local genealogy. (518) 828-5240

Bring a lot of money if anyone in your party is interested in antiques. There are over 20 antique shops on Warrren Street alone.

Tucked away in the northwest corner of town is the American Museum of Firefighting. Dating from 1731, this nostalgic and meticulously restored collection of fire-fighting apparatus has been put together by The Firemen's Association of the State of New York. Open 9 to 4:30 except Monday from April through October. (518) 828-7695

Plan a picnic when you get to Clermont, the home of seven generations of Livingstons, distinguished New Yorkers who contributed much to America's early development and founding as a nation.

Although not identified on the Marine chart, Clermont is about 14 nautical miles south of Hudson, on the eastern shore across from Saugerties and the outlet of the Esopus Creek. Clermont is a State Historic Site and, with lands along 20 miles of eastern shore, is also designated as a National Historic Landmark.

Reach Clermont by anchoring off the road leading from the river up to the hamlet of Tivoli. It's good anchorage but there's no phone, no taxi, and no dock. Watch out for trains. After a short, steep uphill climb, turn left to reach the estate. It's walkable, but a bike would make it a lot easier. There's a bakery, pizza, butcher shop and Mexican restaurant in Tivoli.

Judging from the number of other visitors on the Sundays I've been there, Clermont is one of the most unappreciated historic sites on the Hudson River. The parking lot is sparsely settled; only a few picnic at one of the loveliest views along a lovely river; and never more than four or five others take the guided tour of the house.

The family was founded in America by Robert, a Scotsman reared in the Netherlands--fortuitous childhood for an ambitious lad landing in Dutch-dominated Albany at age 20 in 1674. Intelligent, shrewd and hard-working, he gradually acquired vast estates. Probably because of the Livingstons' strong and early espousal of the patriot cause during the Revolution, the British extended their campaign after burning Kingston in order to burn the original home on this site. It was rebuilt over the next several years, using the foundation and some of the original masonry.

If Clermont sounds familiar in a different context, it's because the first successful steamboat was the product of Chancellor Livingston's partnership with the inventor Robert Fulton. The famous boat was not originally named Clermont but rather "The North River Steamboat of Clermont." Somehow the name Clermont (certainly shorter than North River Steamboat) was popularized for this ship and that's how it was brought down

Clermont, Hudson River manor house of the distinguished Livingston family.

Riverside view of the Vanderbilt estate--one of the Vanderbilt estates!

to us in history. Fulton and Livingston went on to monopolize the Hudson River steamboat trade until their grip was loosened by lawmakers just before the Erie Canal opened.

Looking down to the river from the front yard the location of the long-ago Livingston dock where the Clermont stopped on its historic maiden voyage can be seen at the end of a grassy

148

road, across the railroad tracks. It's a gentle slope compared to many of the other climbs needed to reach historic places sited on these high bluffs. How completely appropriate a small pier would be here, enabling Hudson River sailors to call in at this gem of an historic site. And tie-up where the North River Steamboat of Clermont once docked!

Clermont may be a little difficult to reach for the boater but it's not really daunting. Farther down the river at least three (four if you're a golfer) great destinations can be reached by calling in at the Poughkeepsie Yacht Club. Hyde Park, the Vanderbilt Mansion and the Culinary Institute of America are all close-by to the south of the PYC; Dinsmore Golf Course lies just to the north.

These are all completely different experiences and all are readily accessible from the PYC, which lies just north of Bard Rock on the marine chart.

The Vanderbilt Mansion, you'll find out once you get there,

Roosevelt home at Hyde Park.

149

Tour boat Commander docking at West Point.

is not the only Vanderbilt Mansion. This was a very rich family, with many Mansions, but this is the one that became famous. It is certainly the most visited and always seems to be busy. The grounds are extensive with stunning, absolutely magnificent views of the river. Allow at least a half-day for this visit. Walk the grounds unescorted but by far the best way to understand the mansion and gain a little bit of an insight into the family is to take the escorted tour through the building. But if you're in a hurry and choose not to wait for the guided tour, just read the plaques--they do a lot of explaining--and keep on moving. There's a relevant gift shop right in the mansion--the books, photos, and memorabilia really do relate to the family and the estate. It's about two-and-one-half miles from the Poughkeepsie Yacht Club to the Vanderbilt place. Up-hill, of course, but not too steep. Taxis are available.

If the Vanderbilt Mansion is a monument to a family's fortune, the Franklin D. Roosevelt National Historic Site a mile-and-a-half south at Hyde Park is a monument to public service. This can be a busy place too on any summer day, but this is a rich varied experience. Allow all the time you can. It's so much more than politics because Roosevelt's life transcended mortal accomplishments. It's all fascinating: Roosevelt's early education and careers, family's roots on this land, diverse interests, relatives and cronies. And visitors. You can almost feel the presence of

Churchill walking about the house, waving a big black cigar.

Still a little farther south along the same road is America's premiere training site for world-class chefs: The Culinary Institute of America. Even if you didn't have the foresight to call ahead long, long ago for reservations at the restaurants, it's great fun just to walk around because the students all seem to have such an upbeat attitude. It's a feel-good place.

But if you want to feel really good, call ahead (914) 471-6608 for reservations at any of the four restaurants. There's St. Andrew's Cafe for straight-ahead food with a healthful bent; Caterina de Medici, for -- what else? -- high class Italian; Escoffier for high class French; and American Bounty for regional and American gourmet.

Before you sail out of the Hudson's friendly confines into the open expanses of Haverstraw Bay and the Tappan Zee, join into the rich fabric of military history and tradition at the United States Military Academy at West Point. This is the third most visited tourist attraction in New York and is unquestionably the most friendly for those arriving by boat. If there were an award for the most Boater-Friendly Destination on the Inland Waterways of New York State, it would probably be won every year by the USMA for their thoughtful accommodation of the transient tourist arriving by watercraft. This is not a marina but they do want you to call in -- monitor Channel 13 and 16. (914) 938-3011; 938-2137) Excursion craft are given priority and there are days--Fall football Saturdays--when the excursion traffic is fearsome.

The docks are just south of Duck Island on the marine chart. It's a little bit of a climb--but not too strenuous--up to the campus. As a military installation, this is a "open post" so you are free to roam around and soak up the atmosphere. Everyone seems to visit the Museum at the Visitor Center. Also, buses leave from this spot on guided tours, a great idea for the casual tourist.

Sailors don't have to stop. They can go on forever. But books do have to stop, somewhere.

APPENDIX

Further Readings:
Boating on the Hudson: THE GUIDE, published annually beginning in 1992, contains advertising. Great detail on marinas, boat basins, launch ramps, yacht clubs, nautical facilities. Beacon Publishing Co., 27 Beacon St., Yonkers, NY 10701. $22.92 sold through chandleries and yacht clubs.

Boating Almanac, Volume 3. New Jersey, Delaware Bay, Hudson River, Erie Canal from Waterford to Oswego, Lake Champlain. Annual listing of marinas, repair yards, boat rentals, launch ramps, yacht clubs, Coast Guard stations, with chart references. Contains advertising. Boating Almanac Co., Inc., 203 McKinsey Road, Severna Park, Md. 21146. (301) 647-0084. $10.50 each, plus $2.00 for mail order. Maryland residents add 5% sales tax.

Chapman PILOTING, Seamanship & Small Boat Handling is the most authoritative book in the field. Over 600 pages of valuable information. $23.95. Hearst Marine Books.

Cruising Guide to Lake Champlain, is a very complete and thorough guide with up-to-date information on marinas, restaurants, supplies, groceries, cities and towns, anchorages, and parks. Uniquely illustrated with aerial photos of anchorages, bays, marinas, docks. Contains advertising. $19.95 plus $3.00. Lake Champlain Publishing Company, 176 Battery Street, Burlington, VT 05401. 800-522-0028; 802-864-7733.

Erie Canal Heritage Trail, map of a continuous section in Orleans and Monroe Counties, from the Niagara County line to Wayne County. NYS Department of Transportation--Canals Unit, Region 4; 1530 Jefferson Rd., Rochester, NY 14623-3161. (716) 272- 3490.

Finger Lakes--25 Bicycle Tours, $9.95; 25 Walks, $5.95; Backcountry Publications, P. O. Box 175, Woodstock, Vt. 05091

Finger Lakes of New York State Map, Marshall Penn-York Co., 538 Erie Blvd. West Syracuse, NY 13204. (315) 422-2162.

Foundation for Boating Safety
1-800-336-BOAT

Great Lakes Waterway Guide. Annual listing of principal marine facilities with chart locator. Covers Great Lakes, Hudson River, Lake Champlain, suggested trips on Erie Canal and connecting waterways. Contains advertising. $29.95 plus $3.00 shipping from Waterway Guide, 6255 Barfield Road, Atlanta, GA 30328. Credit card orders: 1-800-233-3359

Hudson Valley is a monthly life style magazine from Suburban Publishing, Inc. Box 429, Poughkeepsie, NY, 12602. $18.00 per year.(914)485-7844.

Hudson River Boating Guide is a real cruising guide with first hand information on piloting and river conditions as observed and documented by an experienced skipper. Also, information on marinas. Advertising. First published in 1992, it is not clear whether this will be an annual. From Hudson River Boating News. P. O. Box 918, North Tarrytown, NY 10591. $12.95 at Walden and B. Dalton bookstores in the Hudson River valley, yacht clubs, marinas (800) 289-4726.

The Hudson River Valley--A History & Guide, by Tim Mulligan, Random House. Outstanding guide for the motorist. Informed comment on restaurants and accommodations.

Hudson--Colonial Restoration Walking Tours, Columbia County Chamber of Commerce, 729 Columbia Street, Hudson, NY 12534. (518) 828-4417

Marine Charts--Distribution Branch, National Ocean Service, Riverdale, MD 20737-1199. Visa and Mastercard orders to (301) 436-6990.

The New York Bicycle Touring Guide, has a series of inexpensive, very useful maps including the Erie-Mohawk and the Hudson-Champlain. Request ordering information from William N. Hoffman, 624 Candlewyck Road, Lancaster, PA 17601

New York Maps--Planimetric and Topographic, Urban and Village/Hamlet, State Atlas, Railroads, Counties. Map Information Unit, NYS Department of Transportation, State Campus Building 4, Room 105, Albany, NY 12232. (518) 457-3555.

New York State, The Complete Map. Map Works, Inc., 2125 Buffalo Rd., Ste. 112, Rochester, N. Y. 14624. $2.50. 716-426-3880; 800-822-MAPS (in New York). Includes directory of parks and points of interest.

NEW YORK'S CANALS & CONNECTING WATERWAYS MAP,CAPTAIN'S LOG, MARINAS, TOUR BOATS, New York State Waterways Maintenance Division, 1220 Washington Avenue, Building 5, Room 216, Albany, NY 12232

NEW YORK STATE CANALS, Recreational Map and Guide...Erie, Champlain, Oswego, Cayuga--Seneca from: NYS Office of Parks, Recreation and Historic Preservation, Agency Building 1, Empire State Plaza, Albany, NY 12238. (518)474-0456

The New York Bicycle Touring Guide, has a series of inexpensive, very useful maps including the Erie-Mohawk and the Hudson-Champlain. Request ordering information from William N. Hoffman, 624 Candlewyck Road, Lancaster, PA 17601

Waterways: New York's Waterfront News, 132 Grand St., Croton-on-Hudson, NY 10520, Tel.(914) 271-6041; Fax (914)271-2673. A monthly tabloid with an amazingly eclectic collection of articles about almost anything happening on the waterways of New York, from the commercial activity of the New York-New Jersey waterfront to the tourist attractions of the Great Lakes. Topical, always interesting, well-written. $15.00 a year.

CHARTERS AND BOATS-FOR-HIRE
ERIE CANAL:
Mid-Lakes Navigation
11 Jordan Street, Box 61
Skaneateles, NY 13152.
(315)685-5722; (315) 685-8500

Collar City Charters
427 River Street
Troy, NY 12180
(518) 272-5341

LAKE CHAMPLAIN
McKibben Sailing Vacations
176 Battery Street
Burlington, VT 05401
802-864-7733/514-286-7113

Vantage Point Yachts
176 Battery Street
Burlington, VT 05401
802-864-7733

Borchert Marine
219 Chemin des Patriotes
St. Charles-sur-Richelieu, PQ
514-584-2017

CANAL AND RIVER CRUISES
American/Canadian Lines, Inc., P. O. Box 368, Warren, RI 02885
(401) 247-0955; (800) 556-7450. A real cruise: 12 days from Rhode
Island to Quebec City and Montreal via the Hudson River, Erie
and Oswego Canals.

Buffalo Charter Inc. Corp.,P. O. Box 928, Buffalo, NY 14240,
(716)856-6696. Dinner, sight-seeing and entertainment cruises
on the Niagara River and Black Rock Canal.

Captain J. P. Cruise Lines, 78 River Street, Troy, NY 12180

(518) 270-1901. Local and overnight cruises to New York City.

Dutch Apple Cruises, Inc., 1668 Julianne Drive, Castleton, NY 12037. (518) 477-5307; (518) 463-0220. Sight seeing and dinner cruises on the Hudson; cruises from the Capital District to New York City with overnight stay at Hotel Thayer at West Point. Lunch, dinner, champagne brunch cruises from downtown Albany and Glen Sanders Mansion in Scotia.

Erie Canal Transportation Co., Clinton Road, New Hartford, NY 13413. (315)735-1755. Short cruise on 36 foot paddlewheel to the pier at Sylvan Beach via canal and Fish Creek.

Historic Hudson River Cruise, from the City of Hudson's Boat Landing. Afternoons and evenings. (518) 828-2661

Hudson Highlands, P. O. Box 265, Highland Falls, NY 10928.(914) 446-7171. All day and shorter cruises in central Hudson to and from West Point, Haverstraw, Peekskill, Bear Mountain. Through October.

Lockport Locks and Canal Tours, 304 Irving Drive, Tonawanda, NY 14150. (716) 693-3260. Frequent two hour cruises capture a lot of history and dramatic lock operations.

Mid-Lakes Navigation Co., Ltd. 11 Jordan Street, P. O. Box 61 Skaneateles, NY 13152. (315) 685-5722; (315) 685-8500. Lake cruises in the Syracuse area and three day cruises from Syracuse, Buffalo, and Troy.

Miss Buffalo, Niagara Clipper, P. O. Box 1623, Buffalo, NY 14240 (800) 244-8684; from Buffalo/Niagara Falls (716) 856-6696 Dinner and sightseeing cruises on canal, Niagara River and Lake Erie.

Pegasus Riverboat Company,40 Riverside Avenue, Rensellaer, NY 12144.(518) 449-2664. Hudson River dinner and sightseeing cruises from Rensselaer.

Sam Patch, 250 Exchange Blvd., Rochester, NY 14608. (716)

262-5661. Lunch, afternoon and dinner cruises on the Genessee River and the Canal, leaving from near downtown Rochester.

The Poplars, Inc. Riverside Drive, Fultonville, NY 12072 (518) 853-4511 Two hour dinner and lunch cruises on the Mohawk River.

The Apple Grove Inn, Route 31E, Medina NY. (716) 798-2323. Mule drawn packet boat cruises on Erie Canal. Sightseeing, dinner, entertainment on western section.

INDEX

159

Brigadier General John Stanwix (65)
Brockport (114)
Bucktail (18)
Buffalo (5), (18), (27), (37), (51), (71), (105), (111), (113), (120), (121), (155-157)
Burgoyne (128), (137), (138)
Bushnell's Basin (110)
Buttermilk Falls (103)
Camillus (78)
Canada (2), (40), (42), (50), (57), (65), (66), (85), (89), (105), (108), (126)
Canajoharie (56)
Captain Jeff's Marina (113)
Carthage (68)
Castleton Boat Club (142)
Catskill (6), (142)
Catskills (6), (33), (71)
Cayuga & Seneca (19)
Cayuga County (80), (83)
Cayuga Island (41)
Cayuga Lake (80), (91), (94), (102), (104)
Cayuga Wine Trail (104)
Cayuga--Seneca Canal (7), (37), (71), (79), (80), (91), (92), (94), (102)
Chambly Canal (85)
Champlain (7), (11), (12), (14), (19), (22), (25), (30), (37), (71), (85), (123), (124), (130-135), (137), (139), (153-156)
Champlain Canal (7), (14), (85), (123), (133), (134)
Champlain, Samuel de (71)
Chateau LaFayette (100)
Chemung (19), (101)
Chenango (19)
Chesapeake & Ohio (4), (12)
Church of Jesus Christ of Latter Day Saints (8), (83)
Clermont (146-149)
Clinton, DeWitt (13), (14), (18), (115)
Clyde (81)
Coast Guard Auxiliary (21), (38)
Coeyman (142)
Cohoes (29), (36), (37), (43)

Cohoes Falls (36), (37), (43)
Collar City Charters (24), (25), (156)
Colonie (43)
Columbia County Chamber of Commerce (145), (154)
Colvin, VerPlanck (131)
Cooper, James Fennimore (88)
Cornell (103)
Corning Preserve (32)
Corning Tower (33)
Crescent (38), (55)
Crooked Lake Canal (92)
Cross Lake (79)
Crown Point (137-139)
Culinary Institute of America (149), (151)
Delaware & Hudson (19), (121), (153)
DeWitt (26), (67), (68), (77)
DeWitt, Simeon (11)
Dinsmore Golf Course (149)
Dresden (92)
Duck Island (151)
Dundee (100)
Dunham's Marina (100)
Dutch (10), (30), (40), (47), (55), (147), (157)
Dutch Walloons (30)
Eagle Harbor (116)
Eastman Kodak (112)
Ellsworth, Colonel E. E. (124)
Empire State Performing Arts Center (34)
Empire State Plaza (22), (32), (155)
Erie Canal Heritage Trail (27), (153)
Erie Canal Museum (68), (77)
Erie Canal Park (78)
Erie Canal Village (26), (66), (67)
Esopus Creek (146)
F. X. Matt Brewing Co. (62)
Fairport (105), (108), (110)
Federal Dam (6), (22), (36), (37), (123), (141)
Federal government (2), (12), (81)
Finger Lakes (4), (7), (8), (19), (71), (76), (79), (80), (86), (91), (92), (94), (95), (98), (99), (103), (153), (154)

Jogues, Father Isaac (55)
Johnstown (55)
Johnson, Sir William (53), (55), (58)
Kateri Tekakwitha (55), (56)
Keil Canal (88)
Keuka (19), (92)
Keuka Lake (92)
King James II (30)
Kingston (19), (85), (142), (147)
Klein Island (75), (78)
Knapp Vineyards (103)
Knowlesville (116)
Lafayette, Marquis de (18)
Lake Champlain (7), (11), (12), (14), (85), (123), (130), (131), (132), (134), (137), (139), (153), (154), (156)
Lake Champlain Maritime (139)
Lake Erie (2), (4), (11), (12), (18), (74), (78), (82), (85), (105), (108), (110), (111), (113), (118), (157)
Lake George (58), (130-132), (137)
Lake Huron (85)
Lake Ontario (4), (7), (11), (12), (19), (71), (74), (76), (83), (85), (86), (88-90), (105)
Lakeshore Winery-Antique/Craft Shop (103)
Lansingburg (43)
Lassellsville (57)
LeMoyne, Simon (76)
Little Falls (18), (47), (50), (51), (60), (59), (60), (111)
Liverpool (74), (75)
Lockport (18), (26), (108), (113), (116), (117), (119), (157)
Lodi (100)
Loyal Order of Moose (63)
Lucas Vineyards (103)
Lycoming (89)
Lyons (81), (82), (105)
Macedon (71), (81), (84)
MacKinnon, Allan W. (142)
Madison County (17)
Madison, James (12)
Marcy Marina (62), (63)
Margaret Reaney Memorial Library (57)

Olean (19)
Oneida (25)
Oneida Lake (11), (19), (26), (47), (51), (68), (71), (86)
Oneida Ltd. Silversmiths (69)
Onondaga County (8), (11), (71), (74), (75), (78)
Ontario (11-13), (18), (108)
Ontario County (83)
Oppenheim (57)
Oriskany (47), (56), (59), (64-66)
Orleans and Monroe Counties (27), (153)
Orleans county (115)
Oswego (8), (12), (22), (76), (86), (153), (155), (156)
Oswego Canal (7), (19), (37), (74), (85), (88), (89)
Oswego County Historical Society (90)
Oswego River (7), (71), (85)
Ottawa (85)
Ovid (103)
Palmyra (8), (81), (83)
Pathfinder Island (88)
Patroonship (30)
Pell, William Ferris (137)
Pendleton (120)
Penmsylvania (4)
Penn Yan (92), (95)
Philadelphia Orchestra (129)
Phoenix (88)
Pittsford (110), (112)
Plane's Cayuga Vineyard (103)
Poplars Inn (55)
Port Byron (80)
Port Gibson (83)
Port Jervis (19)
Poughkeepsie (141), (149), (150), (154)
Poughkeepsie Yacht Club (149), (150)
Power Squadron (21)
Prejean Winery (99)
Pullman, George (115)
Railroads (5), (9), (11), (76), (77), (115), (155)
Reformed Church of America (61)
Reneau (100)

Rensellaer (32), (35), (36), (116), (157)
Rensellaer Polytechnic Institute (35), (36), (116)
Rent Wars (30)
Republican party (18)
Revolution (4), (7), (10), (12), (18), (32), (47), (54), (64), (65), (67), (82), (121), (126), (134), (137), (147)
Rexford (39), (44)
Richardson's Canal House Inn (110)
Richardson-Bates House Museum (90)
Richelieu River (85), (135)
Rideau Canal (85)
Riverview Marine (142)
Robert Fulton (147)
Robert Jenkins House and Museum (146)
Rochester (8), (18), (26), (27), (77), (82), (84), (94), (105), (108), (110), (109-113), (153), (155), (157), (158)
Rochester Museum and Science Center (112
Rockefeller, Governor Nelson A. (32)
Rolling Vineyards (100)
Rome (14), (26), (51), (52), (63-68)
Romulus (103)
Roosevelt, Franklin D. (150)
Rotterdam (26), (42), (51)
Rotterdam Junction (26), (42), (51)
Salt Museum (75), (76)
Sampson State Park (97), (100)
Sandy Hook (18)
Saratoga Battlefield National Park (126)
Saugerties (146)
Savoy (65)
Schenectady (27), (29), (39-42), (44), (45), (47), (50), (51), (55), (59), (62), (71), (86), (117), (142)
Schenectady County Historical Society (41), (45)
Schenectady Yacht Club (39), (40)
Schoharie Creek Historic Site (54)
Schoharie Crossing (26), (55)
Schuyler County Chamber of Commerce (95), (101)
Schuyler, General Phillip (126)
Schuylerville (128), (130)
Scotia (40), (42), (47), (157)

Treman, Allan H. (102)
Trent-Severn Canal (85)
Troy (6), (22), (25), (26), (29), (35-37), (43), (102), (116), (123), (141), (142), (156), (157)
Troy's Town Dock (142)
Tryon County Committee on Safety (56)
Tug Hill Plateau (7), (68), (86)
U. S. S. Ticonderoga (134)
Union College (44)
United States Military Academy (151)
University of Rochester (110), (112)
Utica (14), (17-19), (47), (62-64), (77), (80)
Utica Club Brewery (62)
Utica Harbor (62)
Valcour Island (134)
Valois (100)
Van Alstyne (56)
Vanderbilt Mansion (149), (150)
Vergennes (134), (138), (139)
Verona Beach State Park (69)
Vischer's Ferry (38), (39)
Wagner Vineyards (100)
Washington, George (6), (12), (56), (128), (137), (138)
War of 1812 (2), (7), (12), (13), (134)
Wardell (120)
Waterford (6), (15), (29), (37), (42), (43), (68), (117), (123), (153)
Waterloo (97)
Watervliet (35), (43), (77)
Watkins Glen (7), (91), (92), (95), (97), (100), (101)
Wayne County (26), (27), (82), (83), (153)
Weedsport (79), (80)
Welland Canal (85)
West Canal Marina (120)
West End Brewing Company (62), (63)
West Point (150), (151), (157)
Western Gateway Bridge (40)
Western Inland Lock Navigation Company (11)
White, Canvass (17)
Wickham Vineyards (100)
Widewaters Marina (116), (118)